LEONARDO
ART AND SCIENCE

LEONARDO
ART AND SCIENCE

Note

Leonardo's manuscripts and drawings, all available in the Vincian National Edition (Giunti), are found in the following locations:
the Codex Atlanticus in the Biblioteca Ambrosiana, Milan;
the Anatomical manuscripts and other drawings in the Royal Library, Windsor Castle;
the Codex Arundel 263 in the British Library, London (the former Library of the British Museum);
Forster Manuscripts I-III in the Library of the Victoria and Albert Museum, London;
Madrid Manuscripts I and II in the Biblioteca Nacional, Madrid;
Manuscripts A-M in the Library of the Institut de France, Paris;
the Codex Hammer (former Codex Leicester) owned by Bill Gates, Seattle, Washington (U.S.A);
the Codex Trivulziano in the Biblioteca Trivulziana, Castello Sforzesco, Milan;
the Codex on the Flight of Birds in the Biblioteca Reale, Turin.

The chronology of Leonardo's notes and drawings frequently varies even within the context of a single manuscript. Accordingly, for each image reproduced, the approximate or certain date is given. Unless otherwise indicated, all of the works reproduced here are by Leonardo da Vinci. Where the location is not indicated, the work is in a private collection.

Opposite page: detail of Leonardo's *Annunciation*, variously dated from 1475 to 1480, Florence, Uffizi Gallery

Managing editor
Claudio Pescio

Editor
Enrica Crispino

Graphics
Carlo Savona

Consultation graphics and pagination
Fabio Filippi

Cover design
Paola Zacchini

Translation
Catherine Frost

Texts
Leonardo. Art and Science is made up of contributions, specially revised for this book, coming from the following publications: A. Chastel, P. Galluzzi, C. Pedretti, *Leonardo*, Art dossier no. 12; L. Antoccia, *Il genio telegenico*, article in "Art e dossier", no. 146; C. Pedretti, D. Laurenza and R. Papa, in *Leonardo. Il cenacolo*, Art dossier no. 146, edited by C. Pedretti; C. Pedretti, *Leonardo. The portrait*, Art dossier no. 138; C. Pedretti, *Leonardo. Il disegno*, Art dossier no. 67; C. Pedretti, M. Cianchi, *Leonardo. I codici*, Art dossier no. 100; M. Cianchi, *Leonardo. Anatomy* ("Grandi della Pittura" series).

Visit our website:
www.giunti.it
www.leonardonline.en

© 2000, 2005 Giunti Editore S.p.A.,
Via Bolognese 165 - 50139 Florence - Italy
Via Dante 4 - 20121 Milan - Italy

Reprint	Year
6 5 4 3 2 1	2010 2009 2008 2007

Printed by Giunti Industrie Grafiche S.p.A. - Prato

CONTENTS

Landscape (1473), Florence, Uffizi Gallery.

A CLOSE-UP OF GENIUS

by Carlo Pedretti

On April 15, 1452 Leonardo was born in Vinci, a little village lying in the shelter of a Medieval castle on the slopes of Montalbano. All around the village are gently sloping hills covered with vineyards and olive groves. In the background the broad valley of the Arno opens out, framed on one side by steep heights crowned with the spas of Monsummano and Montecatini, and on the other, beyond the Fucecchio plain, by San Miniato al Tedesco, site of an imperial court at the time of Matilde di Canossa, and the ancient thoroughfare travelled by pilgrims, merchants and prostitutes: the Via Francigena that linked Northern Europe to Rome.

Vinci is halfway between Florence and Pisa. Leonardo was born, then, in a little village apparently far removed from the world but in reality lying at the crossroads of great highways of communication. At the age of sixteen or seventeen he moved to Florence, where his father, notary by profession, apprenticed him to work in Verrocchio's workshop. The road he covered, on foot or on horseback – forty miles or so – is the one that still today runs along the Arno. This same road had very probably already taken him to Pisa, attracted by a strange landscape where the rocky outcrops in the surrounding mountains often take on the primordial features appearing in the background of the Louvre *Virgin of the Rocks*, the first Milanese painting commissioned of him in 1483 when he was thirty-one. Of similar nature is his first known drawing, the landscape dated August 5, 1473, perhaps painted from nature when he was twenty-one. It is a picture of the Arno valley seen from a high viewpoint, above Vinci, perhaps from Porciano, on the road that leads to Pistoia looking toward Pisa and Livorno. And it is perhaps no coincidence that it was precisely in 1473 that the Florentine Studio with its Faculties of medicine and philosophy moved to Pisa.

In Florence Leonardo spent twelve years of systematic study and intense experimentation, soon entering under the protection of Lorenzo de' Medici, almost his own age (1449-1492), a refined humanist, crafty merchant, wise statesman and skillful politician, but above all an incomparably able diplomat: in short, a master of communication.

For the young Leonardo, Lorenzo was an intriguing example of the technique of communication, where the persuasive power of words was based on eloquence and psychology. Inspired by this example Leonardo began to refine his own visual language, adopting a kind of "speaking" painting which, with the *Adoration of the Magi* painted in 1481 at the age of twenty-nine, arrived at the intensely animated gestures and iconic impact of a silent film. This explains Leonardo's precocious ability to capture his listeners' attention with charming eloquence, an innate gift perhaps inherited from his father the notary. It is the same gift that was soon to serve him well in the systematic program of entrusting his thought to written records, as is done today through magnetic recording.

Following the example of Lorenzo de' Medici, Leonardo became a master of communication. A contemporary referred to him as «another Cato» and Giorgio Vasari, a generation later, presents an image of him still vividly alive, but already wrapped in the proverbial veil of legend expressed in anecdote. «And he was again the first», states Vasari, «who, as a young man, spoke of channeling the Arno River between Florence and Pisa». He then adds: «And every day he made models and drawings to enable him to dig out mountains easily, and to tunnel into them to pass from one level to another [...]. And among these models and drawings there was one which he showed several times to many ingenious citizens who then governed Florence, demonstrating how he wanted to raise the temple of San Giovanni in Florence and put steps under it without ruining it». «And so forceful were the reasons with which he persuaded them», Vasari concludes, «that it seemed possible, although each one after leaving, recognized for himself that such a feat was impossible».

All of Leonardo's work as painter and theoretician of painting is imbued with the concept that art should be considered a form of creative knowledge, on the same level as science and philosophy. And still today the lesson taught by Leonardo has the immediate impact of a live broadcast, whether it involves traditional media – still unsurpassed in historical research – or the new electronic technologies, now beginning to show their true worth as indispensable aid to historical research, having developed beyond the initial stage of games used in play.

On the other hand, Leonardo played too, as noted by Sigmund Freud already in 1910: «The great Leonardo, it seems, remained infantile in some aspects his whole life long. He continued to play even as an adult and for this reason too he was at times incomprehensible and disturbing to the eyes of his contemporaries». And as such – disturbing and incomprehensible – he appears even today, five centuries later, since he has been more studied than understood. The genius has been rediscovered, but the man has been lost.

During a visit to Pavia in January 1490 accompanied by the Sienese architect Francesco di Giorgio Martini for a consultation on work then being done on the cathedral, Leonardo, then thirty-eight, was attracted by the ingenious arrangement of the rooms in a famous bordello in that city, and drew the floor-plan as a model "lupanare".

The drawing appears on a page in a manuscript from that time. Only now has another floor-plan for a bordello been identified, sketched by Leonardo in about 1505 on a folio in the British Library's Codex Arundel at London, and put in evidence by the new facsimile in the publication edited by myself for the National Edition of manuscripts and drawings by Leonardo da Vinci (Giunti). Beside one of the rooms sketched Leonardo notes: «Le putte», an abbreviation for "puttane" (whores). Below this he drew a young man seen in profile, standing and with an erection. The little drawing is still visible in spite of attempts made to delete it at some time in the past by rubbing it with a finger dampened in water or saliva.

On another folio in the same manuscript Leonardo recorded a surprising comment on women which seems to allude to his heterosexual experience at that time, when he was a little over fifty: «The man wants to know if the woman will consent to his lust, and believing that she will, and that she feels desire for the man, he asks her for it and puts his desire in practice, and being unable to do so without confessing, confessing he copulates».

On the same folio, at the same time, Leonardo notes: «catena aurea», which is the title of the grandiose Thomist compendium on the Gospels. These are small but sure indicators of how the real Leonardo, viewed in close-up, could finally re-emerge in the new millennium. After dying the first time in France on May 2, 1519, he has died many times over in the writings of posterity – those very writings that proclaimed his immortality.

LEONARDO
ART AND SCIENCE

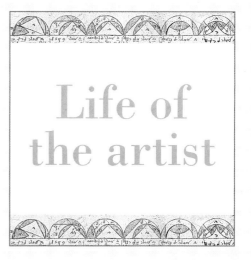

Life of the artist

Almost nothing is known of Leonardo's early education and training. Before his entry into Verrocchio's workshop in Florence in 1469 there is no trace of his talent or of any apprenticeship served in his native Vinci, a little village far from the industrious activity of the artists' workshops in centres such as Florence and Pistoia. Nor do we know of any work of Leonardo completed prior to 1473, the date of the drawing now in the Uffizi.

After this time his career took up off, and he was called upon by powerful States: Milan and Venice, Florence, Rome and the France of King François I. And it was here, on foreign soil, that the life of this extraordinary, complex personality, almost a symbol of the Italian Renaissance, was to come to an end.

Overleaf, on the two preceding pages: Anonymous, Doria Panel (1503-1504).

1. View of Vinci (Province of Florence), Leonardo's birthplace.

2. Seal of the Town of Vinci, 14th century, Florence, Bargello National Museum.

3. The Vincian Museum at Vinci, in Castello Guidi, with models of Leonardo's machines.

4. Florentia (map known as "della Catena"), Florence, c. 1472, Museo di Firenze com'era.

5. Map of Florence by Pietro del Massaio Fiorentino with the most important monuments (1469), Rome, Biblioteca Apostolica.

1

2

3

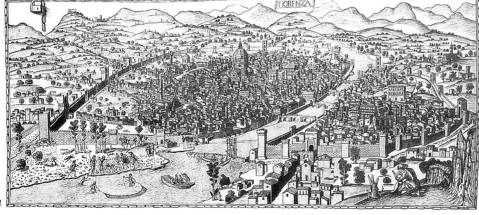

4

≪ 1452 a grandson was born to me, the son of Ser Piero my son, on April 15, on Saturday, at 3 o'clock in the night. He was named Lionardo. He was baptised by the priest Piero di Bartolomeo da Vinci≫. This record of Leonardo's birth in the village that his name was to make famous was noted by his grandfather Antonio, a notary. In Vinci, situated about thirty kilometres from Florence, the artist's family, which belonged to the upper middle class of landowners, had been living since the 13th century. The house of Leonardo's father, where he spent his childhood (and may have been born) still exists today, on the outskirts of the modern town.

Leonardo was the illegitimate son (not a particularly problematical situation, in those days) of Ser Piero and a woman of lower social standing named Caterina. In his writings Leonardo mentions his family and his boyhood only very rarely. At the age of five he was living in the home of his father, who had married in the meantime. As for his education, he himself was later to lament the lack of good schooling, exerting great efforts to learn Latin and geometry. At the death of his grandfather in 1468, Leonardo followed his father to Florence where Ser Piero, who was to have twelve children, moved with the whole family. In the *Cronica rimata* by Giovanni Santi, Raphael's father, – a document published only in the 19th century and then unaccountably forgotten – the exceptional chronicler narrates the stages of a journey to Florence undertaken by Federigo da Montefeltro, duke of Urbino, in that same 1468. In describing the stop in Florence he pauses to list the successful artists of the day, among whom were two rising stars: ≪Two young men the equals in rank and in loves / Leonardo da Vinci and Perusino / Pier della Pieve who is

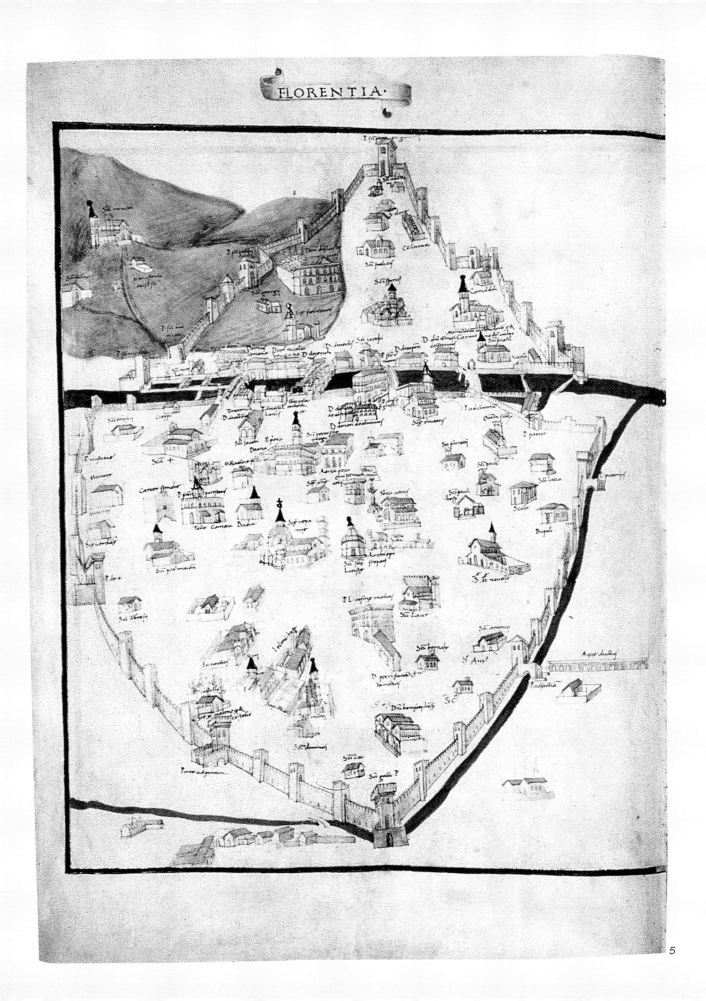

1. *Domenico Ghirlandaio, Approval of the Franciscan Rule by Honorius III, (detail with, from right to left, Poliziano and the three sons of Lorenzo de' Medici:*

Giovanni, Piero and Giuliano) (1485), Florence, Church of Santa Trinita, Sassetti Chapel.
2. *Sandro Botticelli, Madonna with Child, the Infant St. John and two Angels (c. 1468),*

Florence, Accademia Gallery.
3. *Workshop of Andrea del Verrocchio, Virgin with Child standing on a Parapet (1471), Monastery of Camaldoli.*

4. The Virgin *with the Flowers (1478-1481), Munich, Alte Pinakothek.*

1

2

3

a divine painter». In 1468 Leonardo was sixteen years old. A document dated 1469 informs us that he was still living with his father, thus hinting that he may have approached the art of painting even earlier than has been thought, since his entry into the workshop of Andrea del Verrocchio, one of the most famous and popular Florentine artists of the times, is customarily considered to have taken place in 1469. His companions in this precocious apprenticeship were other young painters named Botticelli, Perugino, Lorenzo di Credi and Francesco di Simone Ferrucci.

APPRENTICED TO VERROCCHIO

Why Leonardo turned to the artist's career rather than the notary's profession, in keeping with his family tradition, is unknown. His apprenticeship with Verrocchio, in the city rightly considered the cradle of the Italian Renaissance, gave him an almost complete education in art, with experience ranging from sculpture to painting and architecture, and from the diligent study of figures to the theory of optics and perspective and thus of geometry, natural sciences – botany in particular – and music. Moreover, he had a chance to become acquainted with the great clients, the Medici in particular, who not only preferred Verrocchio's workshop but also used the services of Leonardo's father as the family notary. However, we have no knowledge of any work by Leonardo prior to 1473, the date of his earliest known drawing, now in the Uffizi. It is true that in 1472, at the age of twenty, Leonardo was already enrolled in the Guild of Florentine Painters, the corporation of San Luca, entitled to receive commissions independent of his master, but it is equally true that in 1476 he was still apprenticed to Verrocchio. Perhaps the episode related

1. Angel's head, study for the Baptism of Christ by Verrocchio and Leonardo (1473), Turin, Biblioteca Reale.

2. Verrocchio and Leonardo, Baptism of Christ, (1473-1478) detail of the angel painted by Leonardo, Florence, Uffizi Gallery.

3. Study of hands, Windsor, Royal Library.

4. Verrocchio and Leonardo, Baptism of Christ (1473-1478), Florence, Uffizi Gallery.

5. St. Jerome (1480-1482), Rome, Pinacoteca Vaticana.

1

2

3

4

by Vasari in regard to the angel painted by Leonardo in his master's *Baptism of Christ* (now in the Uffizi Gallery) took place at that time. It even seems that as late as 1478 Verrocchio (often absent from Florence since he had been commissioned to sculpt the equestrian monument to Bartolomeo Colleoni in Venice) entrusted Leonardo and Lorenzo di Credi with the task of completing an important altar-piece for the Pistoia Cathedral. This is the famous *Madonna di Piazza*, from which comes a part of the predella attributable to Leonardo, the *Annunciation* now in the Louvre. Also dating from that time, although not from the same occasion, are the stupendous studies of drapery drawn by Leonardo with brush tip on very fine linen, or with metal tip on red paper.

Perhaps this gave Leonardo the idea of an *Annunciation* adapted to the format of an altarpiece. This is the painting now in the Uffizi. Its style seems to point to the time of his collaboration on Verrocchio's *Madonna di Piazza*, starting in 1478. And in fact a study for the Virgin's raised hand appears on a folio of various studies of hands in the Windsor collection, all of which can be linked to the gesticulating figures in the *Adoration of the Magi*, the painting which first engaged Leonardo on a monumental scale. For this work, commissioned of him in 1481 by the monks in the monastery of San Donato a Scopeto near Florence, the last payment, made on September 28 of the same year, is documented. Upon his departure for Milan the following year Leonardo left the painting unfinished with the father of Ginevra Benci, whose portrait he had painted some years before (now in the National Gallery at Washington). Coeval with the *Adoration of the Magi* is the *St. Jerome* of the Pinacoteca Vaticana which shows spatial effects similar, in

16

1. *Study for a Madonna of the Cat (1478-1480), London, British Museum.*

2. *Study from life for a Madonna of the Cat (1480-1483), Florence, Uffizi Gallery, Gabinetto dei disegni e delle stampe.*

3. *Study for young woman with a child in her arms (1478-1480), London, British Museum.*

4. *Study for a cherub (c. 1480), Florence, Uffizi Gallery.*

5. *The Benois Madonna (1478 -1480), St. Petersburg, Hermitage.*

1

2

3

4

the representation of the human body, to other early works such as the *Benois Madonna* at the Hermitage in St. Petersburg and studies for the lost *Madonna of the Cat.*

FROM THE MAGNIFICENT TO IL MORO

Lorenzo the Magnificent had given Leonardo access to the sculpture garden of San Marco with its precious Medicean collection of antique statues – a collection of decisive importance for the new generations of Florentine artists including the already successful Leonardo and, a few years later, Michelangelo. The protection of Lorenzo the Magnificent was determinant for what was to be the great changing point in Leonardo's career: the move to Milan, another political and cultural capital of Italy at the time, in 1482. This is confirmed by the oldest source on Leonardo, the so-called Anonimo Gaddiano (writing in about 1540), utilised later by Vasari. From this source we learn that it was Lorenzo who sent Leonardo to Ludovico Sforza, known as Il Moro, as his emissary for art (a gesture obviously to be viewed within the broader context of political and diplomatic relations). «He was thirty years old when from the said magnificent Lorenzo he was sent to the Duke of Milan [...] to give him a lyre, which instrument he played to perfection». Leonardo presented himself to Ludovico il Moro with a letter in which he described his skills, including those as civil engineer and constructor of war machines. In the field of art he mentioned an ambitious project which he was never able to carry out: «constructing a bronze horse which will be to the immortal glory and eternal honour of the felicitous memory of your father [Francesco I] and of the illustrious House of Sforza».

In the Lombard capital the artist

1. *Study of animals, detail of St. George and the dragon (1507-1508), Windsor, Royal Library.*
2. *Caricature (c. 1507).*
3. *Study of rearing horse and horseman trampling on a fallen enemy (c. 1490), Windsor, Royal Library.*
4. *Caricature study for head of a man with curly hair (c. 1515), Oxford, Christ Church College.*
5. *Painted decoration of the Sala delle Asse (c. 1498), Milan, Castello Sforzesco.*

1

2

3

4

lived with the De Predis brothers, also painters, in the Porta Ticinese quarter. To the Milanese period belong the *Virgin of the Rocks* in the Louvre, for which there is a contract dated 1483, and the *Lady of the Ermine* now in Crakow, a portrait of Cecilia Gallerani, the mistress of Ludovico Sforza.

In Milan Leonardo continued his assiduous study of the human figure, under every aspect: anatomy, motion, expression (and thus physiognomy), in pictures ranging from portraits to caricature. His folios are crowded with profiles and grotesque figures, in an impetuous succession of types and characters – personages who throng the streets, squares, markets, churches and bordellos.

The years between 1495 and 1497 saw the birth of one of his most famous works, the *Last Supper* in the church of Santa Maria delle Grazie. While working on this fresco Leonardo received a commission to decorate a great hall on the ground floor of the tower on the north-eastern side of the Castello Sforzesco, the Sala delle Asse. This work seems inspired by the festivities held at Milan in 1494 for the wedding of Ludovico Sforza's niece, Bianca Maria, and the Emperor Maximilian. Leonardo had the idea of transforming the hall into an "outdoor" ambience, with a pergola of trees whose branches intertwine along the lines of the vaulted ceiling. The trees (perhaps the black mulberry of the Sforza emblems) are rooted in rocky soil, sectioned in depth as if to reveal the very foundations of the Castello Sforzesco.

The project took on a political meaning. The visual metaphor suggests how good government can be compared to the geometric precision and complexity of Nature's works. In the intricate system of intertwining branches and ropes can be seen, as in good govern-

1. *Study of horses for the* Battle of Anghiari, *detail, Windsor, Royal Library (no. 12326r).*

2. *Map of Imola (1502), Windsor, Royal Library.*

3. *Preparatory drawing for the* Battle of Anghiari, *Venice, Gallerie dell'Accademia.*

4. *Aristotele da Sangallo (attr.), copy of Michelangelo's cartoon for the* Battle of Cascina, *Norfolk, Holkam Hall.*

5. *Anonymous, Doria Panel (1503-1504).*

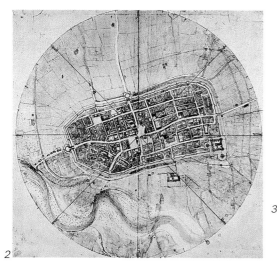

ment, the strength that radiates from a point located at the upper centre: the Sforza coat-of-arms. This was the last work accomplished by Leonardo in Milan. In 1499 the King of France Louis XII invaded the Duchy of Milan: «The Duke lost the state, his property and his freedom, and no work was finished for him», wrote Leonardo in 1500. As events precipitated the artist left Milan and returned to Florence after eighteen years of absence.

In the trip back to Florence, between late 1499 and early 1500, Leonardo stopped at Venice where he was consulted for works of military engineering on the eastern boundary of the Venetian Republic. The painter did not pass unobserved, and admiring comments acclaimed the charcoal portrait of Isabella d'Este drawn by him a little earlier in Mantua. Although it is not known whether he had other works of art with him, it is certain that he brought abundant manuscripts and drawings.

BACK IN FLORENCE

«The life of Leonardo is extremely varied and undetermined, so that it seems he lives only for the day», wrote Piero da Novellara to Isabella d'Este. On the date of April 3, 1501, Leonardo received Isabella's correspondent in Florence. In 1502 he was in Romagna as military architect in the service of Cesare Borgia. The next year he was back in Florence, where he was commissioned to decorate the new Great Council Hall constructed at the back of Palazzo Vecchio from 1495 to 1498. The subject chosen for the painting was a historical one, the battle of Anghiari. The enormous composition (three times bigger than the *Last Supper*) was to commemorate the victory of the Florentines over the Milaneses in 1440. A year later, the central part of the composition had already been

5

1. *Hall of the Five Hundred, Florence, Palazzo Vecchio.*

2. *Drawing of Michelangelo's* David *(1504) detail, Windsor, Royal Library (no. 12591r).*

3. *Study of the course of the Arno (1503), Madrid Codex II (fo. 149r).*

4. *Study of proportions (c. 1490) and study of horsemen for the* Battle of Anghiari *(additions around 1503-1504), Venice, Gallerie dell'Accademia.*

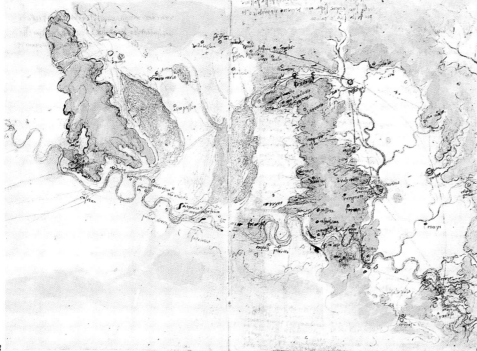

transferred to the wall. In the meantime Michelangelo, already renowned as the sculptor of the colossal *David*, had been commissioned to decorate the other side of the wall. This painting was to have a similar subject, the *Battle of Cascina*, but Michelangelo completed only the cartoon, returning to the Pope's service in 1506. Leonardo too abandoned the work in about 1506, when he departed for Milan at the request of the French governor Charles d'Amboise. And so they disappeared, the two works which for Cellini «while they existed were a school for the whole world». Michelangelo's cartoon was dismembered in 1512 upon the return of the Medici to Florence. Leonardo's painting disappeared in 1563 when the hall was restructured by Vasari. Only copies, prints and drawings remain.

THE SECOND STAY IN MILAN

During his second stay in Milan Leonardo worked mainly on architectural and river channelling projects. In particular, some sketches and notes for a palace and garden designed for D'Amboise near the church of San Babila are known. It was probably after 1508 that the Marshall of France Gian Giacomo Trivulzio requested him to design an equestrian monument to be erected in his funeral chapel built by Bramantino after 1512 in the Milanese church of San Nazaro. The second version of the *Virgin of the Rocks*, in which the figures are more sculptural and the setting more architectural, also belongs to Leonardo's second stay in Milan.

Then came the mythological subjects. *Leda*, symbol of the fecund forces of Nature, appeared already at the time of the studies for the *Battle of Anghiari*, in about 1504, as did another mythological theme, that of *Neptune with his seahorses*. Lastly, the

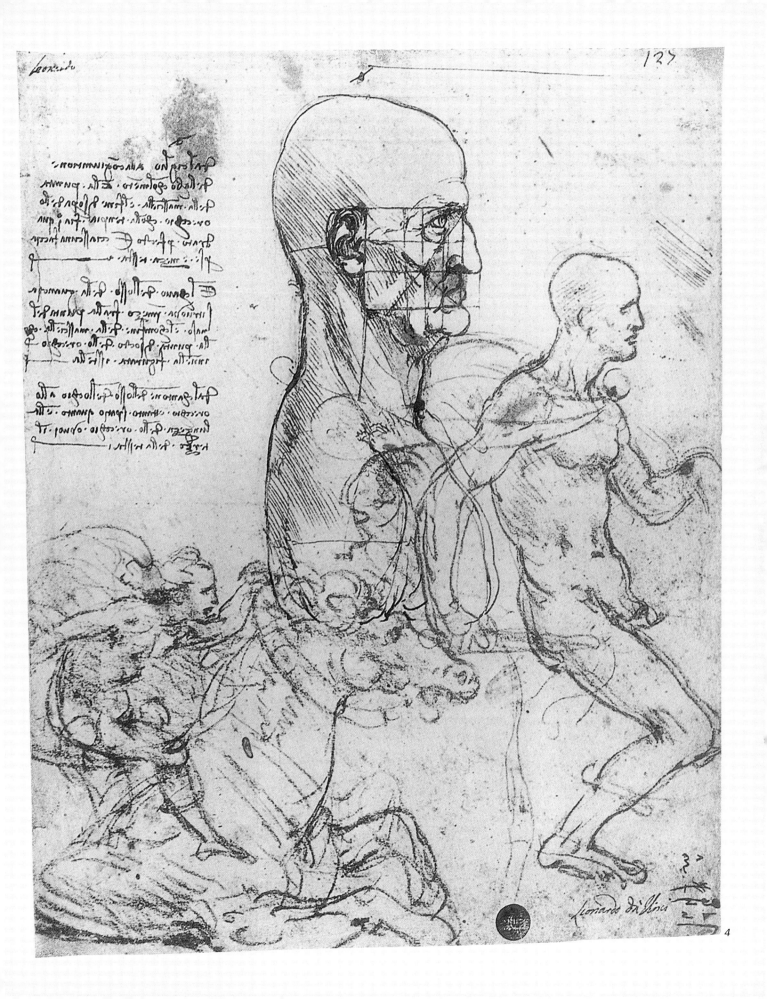

1. Raphael,
Portrait of Leo X
(1518),
Florence,
Uffizi Gallery.

2. Portrait of Lorenzo
de' Medici
(1483-1485),
from the Codex
Atlanticus
(fo. 902 ii r),
Windsor,
Royal Library
(12442r).

3. Anonymous
Lombard painter
(late 14th century),
Sforzesca
Altarpiece,
detail with
Ludovico il Moro,
Milan,
Brera.

4. Jean Clouet,
François I
(c. 1525),
Paris, Louvre.

5. Neptune with
his seahorses,
(c. 1504),
Windsor,
Royal Library
(12570).

1

2

3

4

idea of an angel of the *Annunciation*, known from a pupil's sketch corrected by Leonardo on a folio from the same period, also dates from the time of the *Battle of Anghiari*. Its characteristic features appear again in the *St. John the Baptist* now in the Louvre, datable around 1509.

FROM ROME TO FRANCE

In 1513, the year when Giovanni de' Medici became Pope under the name of Leo X, Leonardo moved from Milan to Rome, with good hopes of receiving commissions through his protector Cardinal Giuliano de' Medici, the Pope's brother. But in Rome Leonardo was to live a rather solitary life in the Belvedere, travelling occasionally to various places. Then in 1517 he accepted the invitation of the King of France who called him to Amboise, honouring him with the highest praise and appointing him «premier peintre, architecte et méchanicien du roi». In the castle of Cloux Leonardo was free to dedicate himself to his research, and here he accomplished the extraordinary drawings of the *Deluge* (now at Windsor). It is probable that his most famous work, the *Mona Lisa*, was also painted during his stay in France.

We know that in France Leonardo was still working on his *Saint Anne*. The studies for the unfinished part of the Virgin's drapery, that which would have revealed through the fabric the mechanics of the positioning of the legs, also date from this period, after 1517. No studies for the *Mona Lisa* exist, but the veils she is draped in show the same characteristics as the studies of drapery done in France for *Saint Anne*. They are veils that model, and thus enhance, the splendid forms they cover, as in the left arm, which can be clearly seen in a a good photograph, up to the elbow and above. Not one of the over forty known copies repro-

5

1. *Woman standing near a stream (Pointing Lady) (c. 1518), Windsor, Royal Library.*

2. *Eye beside a cascade of wavy hair (1515-1516) detail, Codex Atlanticus (fo. 315r-a).*

3. *Telemaco Signorini, Clos-Lucé, (1887), Florence, Uffizi Gallery, Gabinetto dei Disegni e delle Stampe, (no. 96433).*

4. *Photograph of the castle of Cloux (today Clos-Lucé), near Amboise.*

duces this detail. Although dressed, *Mona Lisa* is revealed in the fullness of her anatomical forms.

The same can be said of a charcoal drawing at Windsor from the artist's last years, representing a young woman standing against a landscape of rocks, water and vegetation. Her face, lit by an ineffable smile, is that of the *Mona Lisa*, her hair floats in the breeze, her light garments swirl about her like the clouds in the last drawings of the *Deluge*. One arm is lifted to her breast to grasp the edge of her gown, the other stretches out to indicate a distant point deep in space. If Walter Pater had known of this drawing when he wrote his famous description of the *Mona Lisa*, he would undoubtedly have recognised the same personage as that of the Louvre portrait, whom he had already seen in symbolic relationship with Leda, the mother of Helen of Troy, and Saint Anne, the mother of Mary, almost to suggest that in Leonardo's work – conceptually as well as stylistically – the *Leda* and the *Saint Anne* must necessarily have preceded the *Mona Lisa*. It seems instead that in about 1515 Leonardo was still working on the *Leda*, a small sketch of which appears on a folio of geometric studies from that time in the Codex Atlanticus (fo. 156 r-b).

And on a folio from the same series of geometrical studies, also in the Codex Atlanticus (fo. 315 r-a), datable with precision between 1515 and 1516, appears a pen-and-ink drawing of an eye beside a cascade of wavy hair, just as in the *Mona Lisa*. It is like a graphic reflection, half unconscious, of a hypnotic detail in the painting just completed.

Leonardo died at Amboise on May 2, 1519. His remains, buried in the church of San Fiorentino, were dispersed when his tomb was violated during the religious wars of the 16th century.

1

2

3

4

Among all of the films on Leonardo, *The Life of Leonardo da Vinci* (1971) by Renato Castellani is perhaps the one that achieves the best

A GENIUS IN SERIAL FORM

compromise between entertainment and education.

The story opens with Leonardo dying in the arms of François I. Immediately afterward the narrator, a device employed by the director to provide historical/technical explanations without hindering the free flow of

Upper left, The Hanged Man *(Portrait of Bernardo di Bandino Baroncelli) (1479), Bayonne, Musée Bonnat. Above and below: frames taken from the television serial* Leonardo

the story, interrupts the sequence to announce that this is the somewhat legendary ver-

by Renato Castellani: Philippe Leroy in the part of Leonardo; Leonardo with Ludovico il Moro and Cecilia Gallerani; the friars of Santa Maria delle Grazie standing before the Last Supper.

sion taken from Vasari's *Lives*.

Starting from the very prologue, Castellani thus raises

the question of the mystery surrounding a figure overwhelmingly rich in many-sided aspects («But of the life of such a well-known man what is really known in the end? Very little»).

Crucial moments in Castellani's biographical film are the scene where Leonardo sketches a man hanged for the Pazzi conspiracy in 1478, shocking his friend Lorenzo di Credi, and the one where Leonardo, in the hospital of Santa Maria Nuova, dissects a cadaver to search for «the cause of such gentle dying» – both episodes are metaphors for the thirst for knowledge devoid of any moral scruples even in the face of death.

Leonardo's first years in Milan, marked by the projects for the Navigli and by increasingly fervent studies for the never-to-be-written treatise on anatomy, as well as by a few works of art including the magnificent *Lady of the Ermine*, are convincingly portrayed. In the Leonardo who organised the Paradiso pageant, in frivolous glorification of Ludovico il Moro, Renato Castellani seems to hint at the artist's destiny – yesterday as today – of being forced to produce "pot-boilers" or the works of a courtier to finance his own artistic research.

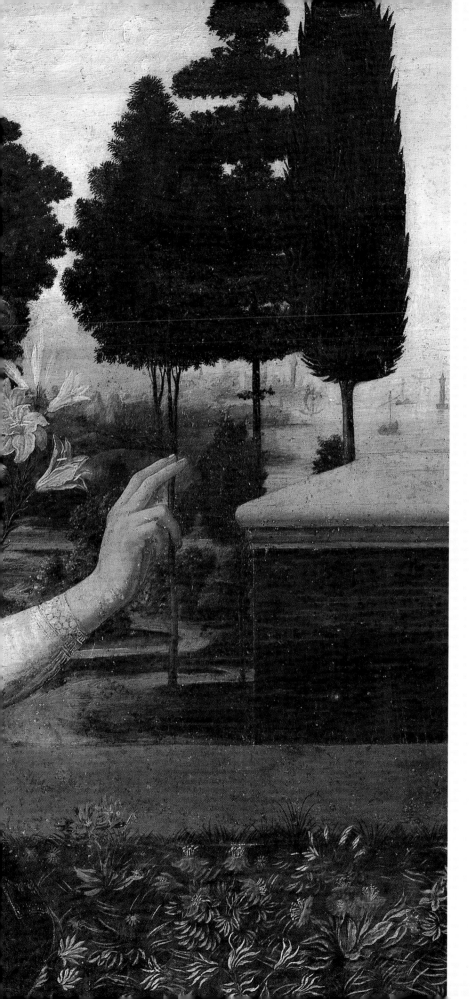

Leonardo's painting

Even a quick glance at Leonardo's artistic production is sufficient to reveal the essence of his work, in the sense of a continuous recurrence to research and experimentation. For Leonardo painting was philosophy, that is, science: the most appropriate language through which to transmit knowledge of the perceivable world. For this reason he could state: «And in effect that which exists in the universe by essence, presence or imagination, the painter has it first in his mind, and then in his hands, and those are of such excellence, that at the same time they generate a proportioned harmony in a single glance, as things do». Art was thus for Leonardo a "second" creation. From his first steps in the Florentine workshop of Verrocchio, the artist matured his research in painting to rise to the supreme heights of the *Last Supper* and the *Mona Lisa*.

Overleaf, on the two
preceding pages:
Annunciation
(1475-1480) detail,
Florence,
Uffizi Gallery.
1. Study from a male
model for the head
of the Virgin in the
Uffizi Annunciation

(c. 1475),
New York,
Pierpont Morgan
Library.
2. Annunciation
(1475-1480) detail,
Florence,
Uffizi Gallery.

3. Verrocchio,
Madonna di Piazza
(1478),
Pistoia Cathedral.
4. Study of drapery
(c. 1478),
Paris,
Louvre.

5. Annunciation
(1478),
Paris,
Louvre.
6. Annunciation
(1475-1480),
Florence,
Uffizi Gallery.

Among Leonardo's youthful masterpieces with religious subjects is the *Annunciation* in the Uffizi. This theme had illustrious precedents, from Simone Martini to Fra Angelico, to the contemporary Antonio Pollaiolo. But in his spatial arrangement Leonardo was still constrained by the scheme of the predella or the bass-relief. He was fascinated by perspective, but committed errors, as in the arm of the Virgin, which cannot reach the book placed on a lectern standing closer to the spectator than the Virgin herself: an error that the splendour of the forms and colours does much to conceal. On the basis of this mistake it has been thought that the painting is a very early one, even from the beginning of the 1470s, but it may be that Leonardo worked on it for years, as if to form a compendium of all of the lessons he had learned. Stylistic similarities between this work and the *Annunciation* in the Louvre, painted by Leonardo for the predella of Verrocchio's *Madonna di Piazza* in Pistoia Cathedral, seem to date it instead after 1478.

Also in the Uffizi is the *Adoration of the Magi*, begun by Leonardo in 1481 and left unfinished when he moved to Milan in 1482. In this case too, the theme is a traditional one. Here Leonardo's spatial arrangement echoes the format of the Ghiberti plaques for the Porta del Paradiso of the Florentine Baptistery, while turning toward the characterisation and animation of the figures in Donatello's bass-reliefs. The painting is little more than a sketch, revealing a creative process emerging as conclusion to lengthy preparatory studies, some of them developed from those for a *Nativity* on which Leonardo was working in 1478, of which nothing more is known. And it is expressly

6

1. *Raphael (attr.), copy of detail on the left in Leonardo's* Adoration of the Magi, *Paris, Louvre.*

2. *Study of horses and horsemen for the* Adoration of the Magi *(c. 1480), Cambridge, Fitzwilliam Museum.*

3. *Filippo Lippi,* Adoration of the Magi *(1496), Florence, Uffizi Gallery.*

4. *Perspective study for the* Adoration of the Magi *(c. 1481), Florence, Uffizi Gallery, Gabinetto dei disegni e delle stampe.*

5. Adoration of the Magi *(1481), Florence, Uffizi Gallery.*

1

2

3

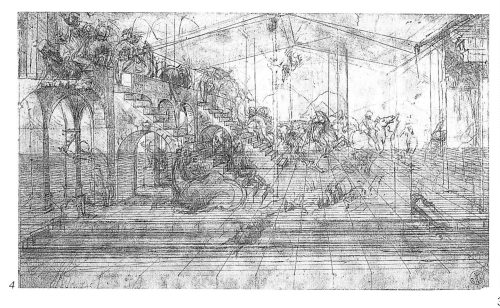

4

the event of the Nativity to be incorporated in the *Adoration of the Magi* in a solution that is highly cinematic. Leonardo employs perspective, which is his movie camera. The composition is centred according to a system of diagonal lines crossing over the Virgin's head. But the perspective of the scene has its vanishing point shifted to the right, between two trees. This means that everything to the right is being left out of the running shot: the hut of the Nativity, where only the ox and the ass remain, partially visible. And this is a way of alluding, with the *Adoration of the Magi*, to the event that had taken place two weeks before, the *Nativity*. Introducing the narration and commenting on it is the young man standing in the right foreground, gazing out of the picture. Even without this proof, he must inevitably be recognised as a self-portrait of the "director", the young Leonardo.

THE SACRED AND THE CORPOREAL

In the figures of the *Adoration of the Magi*, the need for a thorough knowledge of the mechanics of the human body can already be felt. The *St. Jerome* in the Pinacoteca Vaticana, painted in those same years, seems almost an anatomical model, similar to those that Leonardo was to adopt almost thirty years later, in about 1510. But with *St. Jerome* the anatomical model is alive, the form is human, possessing compactness and sculptural shape. It is like a clay model on a circular rotating platform.

Leonardo's first painting in Milan was the *Virgin of the Rocks*, commissioned of him on April 25, 1483 by the Brotherhood of the Immaculate Conception. It seems that the De Predis brothers and some of Leonardo's pupils collaborated on this work.

1. *Virgin of the Rocks (1508),* London, National Gallery.

2. *Marco d'Oggiono or Giovan Antonio Boltraffio, Portrait of a woman (c. 1490),* Milan, Biblioteca Ambrosiana.

3. *Study for the Virgin of the Rocks,* Turin, Biblioteca Reale.

4. Virgin of the Rocks (c. 1483) detail, Paris, Louvre.

5. Virgin of the Rocks (1483-1486), Paris, Louvre.

The very iconography of the group is enigmatic, with the Virgin and Child, the infant St. John and the angel appearing within the enchanted half-light of an incomparable scenario of rocks, water and vegetation. We know only that the theme is the one, hotly debated at the time, of the Immaculate Conception. The angel kneeling to the right, gazing out of the painting, has a function similar to that of the youth standing on the far right in the *Adoration of the Magi*, although it is certainly not a self-portrait of Leonardo, as shown by the study for this figure, now in Turin, portraying a young woman.

On returning to Florence from Milan in late 1499 or early 1500, Leonardo showed a total rejection of painting («He devotes himself to geometry, most impatient with his brush» wrote Pietro da Novellara to Isabella d'Este in 1501). And yet, just at this time, he was creating two works of art weighted with significance for his future development: the first cartoon of *Saint Anne*, lost, and the *Madonna of the Yarn Winders*, known from two versions painted by pupils with the aid of the master. Novellara's letter reports an explanation of the religious symbolism furnished by Leonardo himself. The cartoon of *Saint Anne* is small, but the figures are full size, portrayed seated or leaning. The Virgin in her mother's lap leans toward her son with maternal solicitude, attempting to draw him away from the lamb (symbol of the Passion) which he is joyfully embracing. But Saint Anne tries to dissuade her, and «perhaps indicates the Church which does not wish Christ's passion to be prevented». Preparatory drawings show us how Leonardo proceeded toward the focal point of the iconography, employing effects of scanning and

1. Madonna of the Yarn Winders *(1501)*.
2. *Anonymous, The Virgin, Saint Anne and the Infant St. John, copy from Leonardo.*
3. *Study of woman's bust for the Madonna of the Yarn Winders (c. 1501), Windsor, Royal Library.*
4. The Virgin, Saint Anne, the Child and the Infant St. John, *Burlington House cartoon (c. 1497), London, National Gallery.*
5. The Virgin, Saint Anne and the Child with a Lamb *(1510), Paris, Louvre.*

1

2

3

4

balancing of the forms in relation to the landscape and the architecture. The narration is clear and open; perhaps too open for an iconography which cannot legitimately be presented on a human, almost domestic level. With a sense of classical idealisation of form which is found again in a late cartoon, the one in London, dating from 1508 (as has recently been demonstrated), the iconography is transposed from statement to allusion. It is true that the Virgin is seated in her mother's lap without any apparent tension. But the position of the legs in relation to the twisting of the torso shows that the Virgin could rise effortlessly to her feet and depart, removing her Son from a less obvious symbol of the Passion, his playmate the Infant St. John. But this she does not do. Her mother convinces her by her expression and by the gesture of her hand raised heavenward.

Then came the painting. It is the one begun in about 1510 and now in the Louvre. Leonardo returns to the motif of the lamb, but avoids brusque movements and emphatic gestures. The head of Saint Anne now rises above the group. The Virgin leans forward to support her Son, who has embraced the lamb and turns to gaze at her with an air of glorious triumph. His mother, with her gently melancholy smile, knows that she could take him away merely by raising her head. It is her head, in fact, which keeps her body in equilibrium. The foot of the bent leg, which is not visible, presses against the same rock on which Saint Anne is seated. It is thus the fulcrum of a human balance; but a balance that Saint Anne can control with her concealed hand. The painter has put his science at the service of religious symbolism. At first glance the picture reveals no more than a

*1. Study
for a Bacchus.*

*2. Caravaggio,
Bacchus
(c. 1596-1600),
Florence,
Uffizi Gallery.*

*3. Drawing by a pupil
with the angel
of the Annunciation
on a folio of studies
by Leonardo for the
Battle
of Anghiari
(1503-1505),
Windsor,
Royal Library.*

4. St. John the Baptist
*(1513-1516),
Paris,
Louvre.*

1

2

3

complex, harmonious flow of forms placed before a majestic scenario of mountain chains, an even too obvious allegory of the passage of time.

Painted one year earlier is the *St. John the Baptist* now in the Louvre, datable around 1509. Leonardo's figure, no longer the emaciated one of Tuscan tradition, is florid like a Bacchus, although not openly equivocal as in Caravaggio, of palpitating corporeality, dazzling and at the same time repugnant, his face lit up by a smile that extends to involve the hypnotic fixity of the large eyes encircled in shadow. Already with the *Angel of the Annunciation*, known from a pupil's sketch retouched by Leonardo on a folio from about 1504, Leonardo had arrived at representing the fusion of the sexes: the ambiguity, not merely physical but also mental, of the hermaphrodite. Some school versions exist, the best of which, now in Basil, is attributed to Leonardo.

THE LAST SUPPER

Among the paintings of religious subject the *Last Supper* in the refectory of the monastery of Santa Maria delle Grazie in Milan, Leonardo's most famous painting along the *Mona Lisa*, merits a separate discussion. This fresco was probably painted between 1495 and 1497 – certainly by 1498 as can be assumed from Luca Pacioli's dedicatory letter to Ludovico il Moro, in his *De divina proportione*. For the *Last Supper* the documents of the commission are missing, and thus any indication of planning in relation to the setting and the historical moment. Accordingly, any hypothesis on the creative process can be formulated only on the basis of the hints given by Leonardo himself in his manuscripts and drawings. Very little has remained of the preparatory studies for this monumental work. In

*1. Pages from
Codex Forster II
(ff. 62v and 63r).*

*2. Floor plan of the
Santa Maria
delle Grazie Church.*

*3. First proposal
for interpretation
of the architecture
in the* Last Supper
*as theatrical
stage setting
(Pedretti, 1973).*

4. The Last Supper
*(1495-1498),
Milan,
Santa Maria
delle Grazie.*

one of his pocket-size notebooks Leonardo described the gestures of the apostles, but was still far from any final co-ordination of their actions.

This description/written plan (unique in Leonardo's production) seems almost a kind of screenplay, an action to be used by Leonardo as "painter-director".

It is the proof of a *Last Supper* conceived as a theatrical performance, where the temporal component implied in the gestures of the personages is expressed through spatial arrangement controlled by sources of light – frontal, lateral and background – fusing together in the dynamics of the narration. From this derives the rhythmic scanning of groups of three apostles at the sides of the central figure, isolated, of Christ. If the tracking shot shows how the scene is broken down into episodic sequences, from centre to periphery and vice versa, the close-up is striking for its characterisation removed from context and thus endowed with universal values to clearly reveal the temperament of the personage represented. As for the execution of the work, in this case too Leonardo could have played the role of "director" in the sense that painters from the Milanese academy he founded, such as Marco da Oggiono and Boltraffio, probably collaborated on it.

An indirect confirmation of this is furnished by Giovan Paolo Lomazzo (1538-1600) who mentioned the *Last Supper* in one of his works that remained unpublished up to our own day, the *Libro de' sogni* now in the British Library at London. In an imaginary conversation between the Greek sculptor Phydias and Leonardo, the latter states: «Thus I may hope to say that in drawing and motion I was so perfect in regard to religious matters

4

1. *Andy Warhol,*
   The Last Supper
   (1986).

2. *Giacomo Raffaelli,*
   The Last Supper
   (c. 1806-1814)
   mosaic,
   Vienna,
   Church
   of the Italians.

3. *Romeno Gazzera,*
   The Passion Flower
   (1930).

4. *Study of composition*
   for the Last Supper
   (1493-1494),
   Venice,
   Gallerie
   dell'Accademia.

1

2

3

that many people were inspired by the figures that I had drawn, even before they had been painted by my pupils. Among these figures were those of that Supper in the refectory of the monks of Santa Maria delle Grazie in Milan». It is true that on the scaffolding erected for the *Last Supper*, according to an eye-witness such as Matteo Bandello – we are in 1497 –, Leonardo always appeared alone, but a writer may ignore the presence of assistants in order to heighten the dramatic intensity of his personage.

Leonardo's reconstruction of the episode related in the Gospels is precisely based on the Scriptures. The perspective of the *Last Supper* has in fact a point of view located at a height of six meters – today no longer perceivable, since the flooring has been raised by over a meter – corresponding to the gaze of a man standing on the second floor of a building. Now according to the Gospel writers (Mark, XIV, 15; Luke, XXII, 12), the Last Supper took place in a "coenaculum stratum" (in Greek "anagaion"), that is, a room which in the Mediterranean architecture of the 1st century was located on the second floor of a building.

In representing this scene Leonardo shows that he takes due account of preceding pictorial tradition, while interpreting it freely. In the customary decoration of refectories the Last Supper was almost always part of a broader program that included the other episodes of the Passion. For example, Andrea del Castagno in the refectory of Sant'Apollonia in Florence represented the *Supper* in a building open like a stage , inserted in a birds-eye view of a landscape where the Crucifixion, the Deposition and the Resurrection are taking place.

Now the Milan *Last Supper* has a

4

clear iconographic relationship with the *Crucifixion* painted in 1495 by Giovanni Donato da Montorfano on the opposite wall of the refectory.

It even seems that Leonardo had taken account of the other fresco in the gesture he gave Christ: one hand raised heavenward in the direction of the crucified good thief, the other pointing downward toward the cross of the unrepentant thief.

But there is even more. Before describing the extraordinary animation of the apostles, Luca Pacioli, in 1498, refers to the figure of Christ as «simulacrum of the ardent desire for our salvation». This is a hint at the temporal sequence with which Leonardo was to replace the traditional repertoire of the episodes of the Passion. He incorporates by allusion the theme of the institution of the Eucharist, which in the Gospel of Luke is preceded expressly by the announcement of the sacrifice and is followed by the words that provoke physical and emotional distress among the apostles: «The hand of he who will betray me is here with me on the table». It is no longer important to isolate Judas as had been customary in other representations of this scene. Now he is an actor among the other actors, portrayed with the intense gesture of one who draws back in guilt.

The decision not to isolate the figure of the betrayer may have been influenced by the fact that Santa Maria delle Grazie was a Dominican monastery, and the monks had undoubtedly been consulted as to the iconography of the work. Comparison with other paintings of the Last Supper, in fact, immediately reveals the Dominican nature of Leonardo's biblical exegesis. The *Last Supper* on the *Silverware Cupboard* painted by Fra Angelico for another Dominican

1

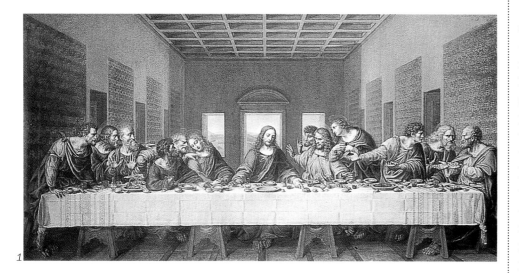

2

1-2. Taddeo Gaddi,
Last Supper
(1350)
whole and detail
of Judas,
Florence,
Santa Croce
Basilica.

3-4. Domenico
Ghirlandaio,
Last Supper
(1480)
whole and detail
of Judas,
Florence,
former Monastery
of Ognissanti.

5. Andrea del
Castagno,
Last Supper
(1450),
Florence,
Refectory
of Sant'Apollonia.

6. The Last Supper
(1495-1498)
detail of Judas,
Peter and John
(in the middle),
Milan,
Santa Maria
delle Grazie.

1

2

3

4

5

monastery, that of San Marco in Florence, has in common with Leonardo's the theological context within which the figure of Judas is interpreted, represented as participating in the Paschal banquet in the same way as the other apostles, he too wearing a halo and recognizable only by the gesture of dipping his bread, as narrated by Mark (XIV, 20).

Conversely, in the Last Suppers painted by Taddeo Gaddi (1350, Florence, Santa Croce), Andrea del Castagno (1450, Florence, Santa Apollonia) and Domenico Ghirlandaio (1480, Florence, Ognissanti), Judas is placed on the opposite side of the table from the other apostles, already isolated and condemned, portrayed as the only one without a halo and with the bag of thirty pieces of silver.

Now a cardinal point in Dominican preaching was the question of free will. In Leonardo's *Last Supper* Judas is shown with the bag of coins, an attribute which distinguishes him, but not isolated nor marked by the absence of a halo, since none of the other apostles have one either. On the contrary John, Jesus' favourite apostle, is placed almost at the same point as Judas. Leonardo depicts Judas as a man torn by indecision, according to the Thomist teaching of the voluntary nature of sin. Judas is condemned for having voluntarily betrayed and above all for having voluntarily despaired in God's pardon.

Accordingly, emphasis is placed on the theme of man's freedom, implicitly replying to the many paintings where, isolated on the other side of the table set for the Easter banquet, could seem the helpless victim of a condemnation "ab aeterno".

As previously mentioned, in the *Last Supper* the apostles are placed in groups of three, six to the right and six to the left of Jesus. In a highly

6

1. *Study for the head of Bartholomew for the* Last Supper *(c. 1495), Windsor, Royal Library.*

2. *Study for an apostle (c. 1495), Windsor, Royal Library.*

3. *Study for the head of Judas for the* Last Supper *(c. 1495), Windsor, Royal Library.*

4. *Study for the heads of Judas and St. Peter for the* Last Supper *(c. 1495), Milan, Biblioteca Ambrosiana.*

5. *The* Last Supper *(1495-1498) detail with Thomas, James the Elder and Philip, Milan, Santa Maria delle Grazie.*

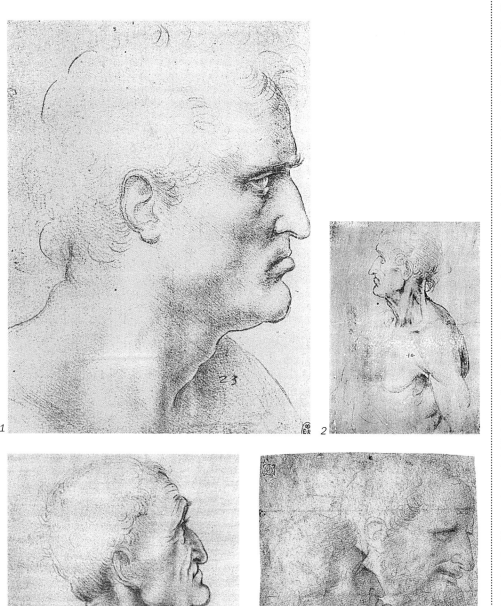

dynamic scene each apostle is represented in his own individual nature, surprised in an attitude that characterises him psychologically in the role he plays in the sacred performance, as related in the Gospels. Examination of the components involved in the iconography of the personages is sufficient alone to reveal the enormous work and complex elaboration faced by Leonardo in creating the *Last Supper*. At least three components form the basis for Leonardo's iconography: tradition, verisimilitude, and the most original aspect, research in anatomy and physiognomy.

As regards the first component, the essential source for the iconography of these personages is primarily the hagiographic tradition, from the Gospels to a work such as the *Vita de santi* by the Camaldolensian Niccolò Malermi, published in the vulgar tongue in 1472. In the second place Leonardo undoubtedly drew inspiration from persons encountered in the streets and in places such as markets, ghettos and synagogues, frequented by Semitic types. There exist notes by Leonardo himself, schematic reminders that reveal his sources, as when he notes: «Christ. Giovan Conte, the man of Cardinal del Mortaro», or «Alessandro Carissimi da Parma, for Christ's hand». And still further: «Giovannina, fantastic face, lives at Santa Caterina, at the hospital». This is in a notebook datable just from the time of the preparatory studies for the *Last Supper*, around 1493-1494. But an even more determinant contemporary testimonial exists, that of Antonio De Beatis who visited the *Last Supper* in 1517, after having met Leonardo at Amboise. It may even be that what he states in his *Diario* was confirmed by Leonardo himself: «The personages in the painting are the natural portraits of several persons in

1. *The shadow of Leonardo projected on the floor (1492) detail, Manuscript A (fo. 1r).*

2. *Scheme of interpretation for the manuscript (Pedretti).*

3. *Andrea del Verrocchio and Leonardo, Bust of Christ (c. 1475).*

4. *Study for the Apostle Philip, Windsor, Royal Library.*

5. *The* Last Supper *(1495-1498) detail with Philip, Milan, Santa Maria delle Grazie.*

1

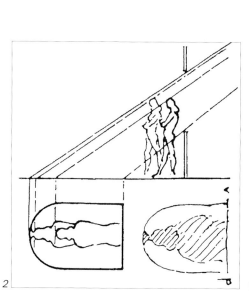

3

2

4

the Court and of Milanese of that time of the same rank», that is, that the figures appearing in the *Last Supper* are portraits of members of the Sforza court. This testimony should not be disregarded, considering also that the figures, of more than life-size, seem drawn from projected shadows, a procedure well known to Leonardo according to Sabba da Castiglione, who in his *Ricordi*, published only in 1546, wrote that Leonardo was reputed to be the «first inventor of the large figures taken from the shadows of lanterns».

As for the third component, Leonardo fused the hagiographic tradition and the search for verisimilitude with his studies of anatomy and physiognomy.

Pliny in his *Naturalis Historia* describes the artist Aristides in these terms: «Aristides was the first among all painters to paint the soul, both the sentiments, which the Greeks call "ethos", and the emotional turmoil». The distinction is clear. It is one thing to represent the permanent character of an individual (which may tend more toward anger or toward timidity, and so on), and it is another to portray the fleeting emotion felt on occasion. Even before Pliny, Aristotle in his *Poetics* referred to the former as "ethos" (permanent characteristic), to the latter as "pathos" (temporary emotion). This distinction is a fundamental key to understanding Leonardo's *Last Supper*, in which he has depicted the instantaneous emotional reaction ("pathos") of the apostles to Christ's announcement that a traitor is among them.

The momentary passion in question is basically the same, a mixture of astonishment, incredulity and fear, but the way in which it is expressed varies from one apostle to another, according to the character ("ethos")

1. *Caricature study of an old man (1490-1495) recto, Rome, Gabinetto nazionale delle stampe e dei disegni.*

2. *Caricature study of an old man (1490-1495) verso, Rome, Gabinetto nazionale delle stampe e dei disegni.*

3. *Study of physiognomy of two profiles, Windsor, Royal Library.*

4. *Two busts of men facing each other (1495), Florence, Uffizi Gallery,*

Gabinetto dei disegni e delle stampe.

5. *Study for the Last Supper (1493-1494), Windsor, Royal Library (no. 12542r).*

1

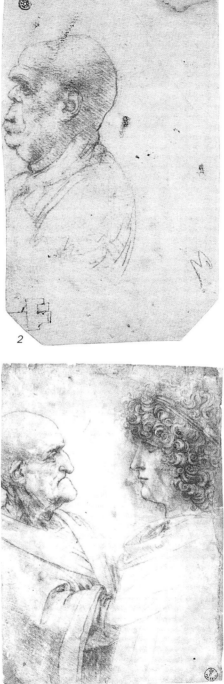

2

3

4

of each. 15th century artistic theory had been deeply concerned with temporary emotions, «movements of the soul» as Alberti called them; less so with permanent character (and not from the viewpoint of physiognomy), and still less with the complex relationship between them. Leonardo carried on this tradition, went deeper into it, and revolutionised it in two ways. First, by basing portrayal of permanent character on scientific considerations of anatomy and physiognomy having to do with the relationship between body and soul. Second, by considering, after having distinguished between them, the complex relationship between "ethos" and "pathos", between physiognomy and momentary passions, «mental motions» as he called them.

Under one of the preparatory drawings for the *Last Supper* (Windsor 12555r), perhaps representing Judas, the artist wrote: «When you draw a figure, consider well who it is and what you want it to do». «Who it is», that is its character, its psychological and somatic nature, its physiognomy; «what you want it to do», that is the momentary emotional participation in the event experienced on the occasion.

Leonardo conceived of physiognomy and momentary passions as part of his anatomical research. The years in which the *Last Supper* was painted as well as the preceding ones (around 1495-1498, but perhaps even earlier) were marked by intense anatomical studies. Dating from 1489 are a group of studies dedicated to the structure of the skull. Leonardo had dissected a cranium, had traced a series of lines relating to precise protuberances and cavities in the bone, and at their meeting point had placed "common sense". This as not only a psychological faculty of sensorial perception

1. *Series of drawings
on the ventricles
of the heart
(1513) detail,
Windsor,
Royal Library
(RL 19118-19119v;
K/P 116v).*

2. *Study for the head
of the Apostle Simon
for the* Last Supper
*(c. 1505),
Windsor,
Royal Library.*

3-4. *Studies of a skull
(1489),
Windsor,
Royal Library.*

5. *The* Last Supper
*(1495-1498),
detail of Matthew,
Milan,
Santa Maria
delle Grazie.*

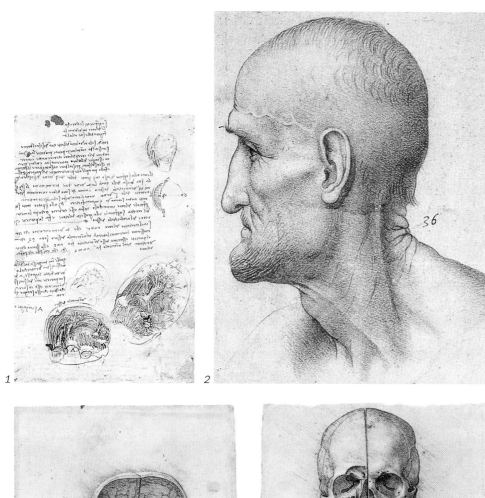

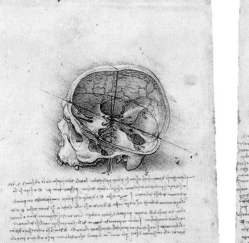

1

2

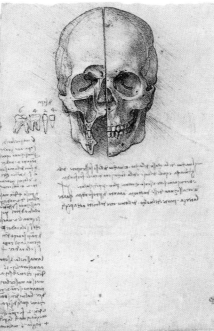

3

4

and the origin of voluntary neuro-muscular movement, but in Leonardo's view it coincided with the very "soul".

The position of the soul is thus closely related to the shape of the body, that of the cranium and its cavities in particular. Apart from this solid, morphological aspect, the relationship between body and soul also had, according to Leonardo, a more fluid substratum: the complexion, the blood, and the heart. While widely-accepted traditional medical theory attributed importance to four different humours – blood, yellow and black bile, phlegm – Leonardo believed that the psychosomatic make-up of an individual depended essentially on one of the humours alone, blood. The connection between body and soul, of physiognomic or emotional type, thus had for Leonardo a dual anatomical basis: morphological (the cranium) and fluid (the heart and blood).

One of his first and most intense studies for the *Last Supper* is a drawing now in Vienna (c. 1490). The firm lines of the cranium, its height, its shape, and even the particular three-quarter foreshortening, are very closely reminiscent of his studies of the skull. But as we know, along with this aspect of studies of the cranium, of morphology and physiognomy, there exists a more fluid one, based on the complexion, which could be more or less sanguine and «spirited». In a preparatory study for the Apostle Simon, known through copies, a vein stands out across his forehead.

Within the context of the fluid and the complexion, the main physiognomic and artistic sign was however colour. And considering the vicissitudes undergone by the *Last Supper* it would be useless to search for traces of it in the work.

5

1-2. The Last Supper
(1495-1498),
detail before and
after restoration,
Milan,
Santa Maria
delle Grazie.

3. First idea
for the figure
of the Apostle Peter
(c. 1490),
Vienna,
Graphische
Sammlung Albertina.

1

2

All of this concerns the physiognomic features of each individual apostle, his character and permanent somatic aspect. On this depends the specific "pathos" of each figure, the emotional reaction to the announcement of betrayal, expressed through gestures and actions, facial expressions, changes in flesh tones.

While the latter are now illegible, as regards facial expressions we can start from the two apostles immediately to the right of Christ: John and Peter. These two personages represent a typical case of convergence between personal research in anatomy and physiognomy and hagiographic tradition, where John's gentle nature (symbolic, according to St. Thomas, of the contemplative life) was frequently opposed to Peter's irascible character (symbolic of active life).

Leonardo, by placing the two disciples one beside another, accentuates the difference through the contrasting features of the two, with an outraged profile appearing beside a melancholy one. John, who according the Gospels was almost resting on Christ's breast when Peter questioned him as to the words pronounced by their Master, is portrayed in gestures consistent with his character: his head gently leaning to one side, his hands clasped in abandonment. Peter, on the contrary, shakes John with his left hand to question him, while with an awkward gesture of the other arm he grasps – almost concealed – a knife. The *Last Supper*, famous and widely copied since the time it was painted, has greatly deteriorated over the years, becoming at last almost illegible. The first attempt at conserving it dates from the early 18th century; the most recent, an endeavour lasting twenty years, was concluded in June 1999.

3

*1. Anonymous
of the 16ᵗʰ century,
Leda,
(1500-1510),
copy from
Leonardo,
Rome,
Galleria Borghese.*

*2. Study for a
"Kneeling Leda"
(1503-1504),
Chatsworth,
Duke of Devonshire
collection.*
*3. Kneeling lady,
(c. 1483), detail,
Bayonne,
Musée Bonnat.*

*4. Master of the
Sforzesca Altarpiece,
Sforzesca
Altarpiece, detail
with portrait
of Beatrice d'Este
(1494),
Milan,
Pinacoteca di Brera.*

*5. Anonymous
of the
16ᵗʰ century,
Leda,
(1506-1508),
copy from
Leonardo,
Florence,
Uffizi Gallery.*

THE MYTHOLOGICAL SUBJECTS

Leda, symbol of the fecund forces of Nature, appeared already at the time of the studies for the *Battle of Anghiari*, around 1504. At first Leonardo imagined her in the kneeling position of the young *St. Jerome*, surrounded by flourishing vegetation which emphasised her exuberant sensuality.

Later, perhaps in Milan, he was to elaborate the standing version. In around 1515, it seems, Leonardo was still working on the *Leda*, of which a small sketch exists on a folio of geometric studies from that time in the Codex Atlanticus (fo. 156 r-b).

Another mythological subject was that of *Neptune with his sea-horses*, where spiral shapes are used to embody the concept of the whirling, twisting forces of nature.

The original motif, inspired by the oval of an ancient gemstone, dates back to 1504, to the time of the *Battle of Anghiari*. Later, the motif of the erect position was to predominate: a figure no longer concentrated in action, but powerful in its Herculean proportions as a warrior in the lost Battle. It is perhaps an idea for a fountain.

THE PORTRAITS

During his stay in Milan, from 1483 to 1499, Leonardo painted at least four portraits, all half-bust views as may have been the sculptures he executed during his apprenticeship with Verrocchio, when he probably acquired experience in the technique of bass-relief as well. It may also be that in the works of Verrocchio himself his pupils or assistants participated, raising a complex problem destined to remain unresolved in the absence of documentary proof. It has thus been hypothesised that Leonardo partici-

1

2

3

4

1. *Andrea del Verrocchio, Noblewoman with Bouquet (c. 1475), Florence, Bargello National Museum.*

2. *Study of hands (1475-1480), Windsor, Royal Library.*

3. *Integration of the emblem of Ginevra Benci (from Thiis, 1909).*

4. *Emblem on back of the Portrait of Ginevra Benci (c. 1475), Washington, National Gallery.*

5. *Mutilated Portrait of Ginevra Benci (c. 1475), Washington, National Gallery.*

pated in the extraordinary marble bust of the so-called *Lady of the Beautiful Hands*, or *Noblewoman with Bouquet* now in the Bargello.

This masterpiece by Verrocchio presents the motif of the hands raised to the breast in an attitude entirely similar to what must have been that of Leonardo's *Portrait of Ginevra Benci*, a work datable around 1475, or even later, and thus still influenced by Verrocchio. The painting is evocative of a sculpture, although the human figure is delicately fused with the symbolic landscape surrounding it (the juniper bush in the background of the diaphanous image alludes to the girl's name). Proof that all of the lower part of Ginevra's portrait that contained the hands is missing is provided by the mutilated emblem on the back of the panel, since it has been possible to establish exactly how much space it would take if complete.

Still of Tuscan imprint, still sculptural is the portrait of the *Musician* in the Ambrosiana, which dates from the first decade of Leonardo's stay in Milan, around 1490. The three-quarter bust viewed slightly from above, the hand holding the sheet of music which emerges from below, the brilliant red of the robe and head-dress, the rosy complexion and the uniformly dark background evoke a Nordic model imported by Antonello.

The bony face is dominated by large glassy eyes, on which the painter's attention was focused. The *Musician*'s eyes have, it can be said, been a school to artists. And they were to return, regularly, in the paintings and drawings of Leonardo's Lombard pupils, Marco da Oggiono and Boltraffio in particular.

In the *Lady of the Ermine*, identified as Cecilia Gallerani, the mistress of Ludovico Sforza, it is impossible to

determine the extent to which the model has been idealised, so that the extraordinary effect of the physiognomic relationship between woman and animal could be entirely real, and could at the same time be symbolically appropriate. In fact the ermine, in Greek "galè", alludes firstly to the family name of the sophisticated courtesan, and is also a traditional symbol of moderation and candour of sentiments. Moreover, this animal was a Sforza symbol, alluding to Ludovico il Moro himself, who in the poetic metaphor of Bellincioni appears in fact as «the Italian Moore, with ermine». And it has recently been discovered that Ludovico greatly desired to be invested with the Order of the Armellino by the King of Naples, the highest honour granted to personages such as the King of England and the Duke of Urbino, an honour of which the Duke could finally boast in 1488, only to renounce it forever in about 1490, when the first conflicts with the Aragonese broke out.

Leonardo's portrait can thus be dated during that period. The date is confirmed by the Spanish costume which came into fashion just at that time, and which dates at the same time the style of an allegorical drawing by Leonardo representing the fable of the ermine, probably designed for a medal.

The *Lady of the Ermine* is a typical example of the so-called "shoulder portrait", a type developed through Leonardo's studies on the dynamics of the human body, as exemplified by the bust of a woman portrayed in eighteen different positions on a folio in the Windsor collection. Cecilia Gallerani, the beautiful, highly educated favourite of Ludovico Sforza, appears in half-bust. Viewed in three-quarter profile looking to the left, she turns to gaze out of the picture to the

1. *Raphael,*
Maddalena Doni
(c. 1506),
Florence,
Galleria Palatina.

2. *Raphael,*
Lady with a Unicorn
(c. 1506),
Rome,
Galleria Borghese.

3. Portrait of Isabella
d'Este
(1500),
Paris,
Louvre.

4. *Anonymous,*
copy of cartoon
for the Portrait
of Isabella d'Este
(XVI century),
Oxford,
Christ Church
College Collection.

5. La Belle Ferronnière
(1495-1498),
Paris,
Louvre.

1

3

4

right, her face exposed to the light that falls on her shoulders and on the white mantle of the ermine she holds in her arms like a cat. Her gaze is intense and slightly detached, her lips barely touched by a smile.

Another extraordinary and still unjustly underrated portrait of a woman is the picture in the Louvre known as *La Belle Ferronnière*, whose style indicates dating at the time of the *Last Supper* or immediately afterward.

The figure appears in a three-quarter view behind a parapet against a dark background. Contrary to what might be expected from Leonardo her arms are not raised to her breast where the hands could be shown even if only to display their beauty. The position of the figure is disconcerting, like that of a person standing for a moment at a window or seated in a box at the theatre and watching those around her. The fascination of this portrait lies in the magnetic fixity of the eyes. «The eye is the window of the soul», stated Leonardo in his *Libro di pittura* where he confronted all theoretical aspects of portrait painting in texts dated mainly from the Sforza period, the time when these portraits were painted. If this is, as seems probable, the portrait of Lucrezia Crivelli, the lady who was to succeed Cecilia Gallerani in the favour of il Moro, and thus in about 1497, this would be an extraordinary experiment in poetic function, which sees in the eyes a source of light, the manifestation of the soul as simulacrum of divinity.

In 1500 Leonardo was back in Florence. From Milan he journeyed to Venice, stopping in Mantua where Isabella d'Este asked him to paint her portrait, which he immediately drew in charcoal, promising her to transfer it to a panel as soon as possible, a promise he was never to fulfill.

1. *School of Leonardo,*
   Nude Gioconda
   (c. 1515),
   St. Petersburg,
   The Hermitage.
2. *Salai and Leonardo,*
   Nude Gioconda
   (c. 1515).

3. *Lorenzo di Credi,*
   Portrait
   of a Young Woman
   (*or* Lady
   of the Jasmine),
   Forlì,
   Pinacoteca
   Civica.

4. *Flemish Master,*
   Portrait of a Lady
   from a cartoon
   of the Leonardesque
   school (c. 1515),
   Rome,
   Galleria Doria
   Pamphilj.

5. Mona Lisa
   (1506-1510;
   1513-1516),
   Paris,
   Louvre.

1

2

3

4

Isabella, the sister of Beatrice, the Duchess of Milan who died in child birth in 1497, appears in a three-quarter view behind a parapet like *La Belle Ferronnière,* but with her face shown in full profile as if on a medal. A hand too can be seen, emerging from below like that of the *Musician,* and laid on the other which can barely be seen and which may have been pointing to a book. This circumstance is confirmed by a poor copy now at Oxford. In 1497 Isabella had had the portrait of Cecilia Gallerani sent to her so that she could compare it with one by Costa.

Although she must have been well aware of Leonardo's subtle innovative quality as portrait painter, she approved a representation of herself that is traditional, tranquil, almost archaic. But if she did so it is because the image, splendidly majestic, already shows the imprint of the new century which was opening with the imperial visions of popes and monarchs and which saw the lesson of antiquity reappearing in republican ideals.

Leonardo's most celebrated portrait, however, and one of the most famous of all times, is the *Mona Lisa.* In all probability this was the painting that Leonardo showed Cardinal Louis of Aragon in France in 1517 as the portrait of «a certain Florentine woman, done from life, at the instance of the late Magnificent, Giuliano de Medici», as reported in that same year by Antonio De Beatis. It is known that Leonardo was in the service of Giuliano from 1513 to 1516, although there may have been earlier contacts, not in Florence, where Giuliano returned from exile only in 1512, but almost certainly in Venice in 1500 where Giuliano was living at he time of Leonardo's brief stay. But any conjectures in this regard would be

*1. Study for
a landscape
(c. 1500) detail,
Windsor,
Royal Library.*

*2-3. Two studies
of drapery for the
Louvre* Saint Anne
*(c. 1518),
Windsor,
Royal Library.*

*4. First reproduction
of the* Mona Lisa
*as illustration
for a chapter
in the French edition
of Leonardo's*
Trattato della pittura
(1651).

*5. Portrait of a maiden
(La Scapiliata)
(c. 1508),
Parma,
Galleria Nazionale.*

hazardous; and it is no longer necessary to anchor the *Mona Lisa* to a time, around 1505, when Raphael could have drawn inspiration from it. At that time in fact the "external" formula of the *Mona Lisa* had already been diffused through Leonardo's other works, as can be seen for example in the portrait of a woman by Lorenzo di Credi at Forlì. The "internal" formula instead was unique and unrepeatable.

In realty the style, elements such as the nature of the landscape and the skilful play of veils seem those of Leonardo's last works, after 1510 – as suggested by Kenneth Clark – and it is probable that the artist continued to work on the painting up to his last days in France.

The French studies – black on black – for the drapery of the Virgin in the painting of *Saint Anne* and the related drawings at Windsor, which date from 1510 and 1511, spring to mind; or the landscapes of the Adda from 1513 and others sketched on folios of geometric studies from 1514 and 1515. On a folio of geometric studies in the Codex Atlanticus (fo. 315r-a), datable with certainty between 1515 and 1516, appears a pen-and-ink drawing of an eye beside a cascade of wavy hair, just as in the *Mona Lisa*, sketched as if inspired by a remembered detail in the just finished painting.

But the most compelling reference is to the character, if not the spirit, of a drawing at Windsor – a very late one – of a woman standing in a landscape that is barely visible in the mist. She has the body, the clothing and even the smile of the *Mona Lisa*; her pointing hand indicates a symbolic distance in space and in time.

Over the *Mona Lisa*, the proverbial rivers of ink have flowed. The painting is a victim of too much erudition,

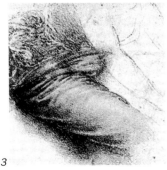

1

2

3

4

1. Antonie van Dyck, Multiple Portrait of Charles I (1635-1636), Windsor, Royal Collections.
2. Giorgione, The three Ages of Man

(1477-1510), Florence, Galleria Palatina.
3. Three views of the same head (c. 1500), Turin, Biblioteca Reale.
4-5. Repertoire of

noses, illustration for a text in the Libro di pittura *(copied from the lost* Libro A, *1508-1510), from the Codex Vaticano Urbinate 1270*

(fo. 108 v), Rome, Biblioteca apostolica vaticana.
6. Portrait of a Musician (c. 1490), Milan, Pinacoteca Ambrosiana.

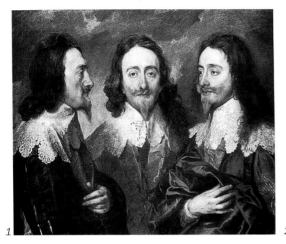

1

2

3

too much philology, too much philosophy, too much psychology, too much arrogance and, on the whole, too much misunderstanding.

Many hypotheses have been formulated as to the identity of the woman portrayed. In 1625 Cassiano dal Pozzo saw the painting at Fontainebleau and christened it "La Gioconda" on the basis of a description by Vasari, who wrote of it with great eloquence, but without ever having seen it. Today it is certain that this is not the Mona Lisa described by Vasari, also in consideration of the previously mentioned testimony of De Beatis.

Perhaps the day may come when the *Mona Lisa* will be wisely restored (but perhaps it would be even wiser to leave her untouched) to bring back the luminosity of Leonardo's colours, intense and vaporous in the distance, brilliant and effulgent in the monumental presence in the foreground. And it can then be confirmed that the key to reading the painting consists expressly of the play of veiled forms: that miraculous «veil of colours» insistently mentioned in the *Trattato della pittura* which modern critics have misunderstood, interpreting it as «relationships between colours». And in the meanwhile the most famous painting in the world will continue to arouse hypotheses and arbitrary inferences. The expression of the face and certain characteristics of the hands have even led to the suggestion that the woman portrayed is pregnant. And of all the interpretations that have been made, from the morbid enthusiasm of 19th century decadence down to the most recent computerised studies, this is perhaps the one most consonant with what is known of Leonardo in his last years. It falls within the context of his embryological studies of 1510-1513 and geological ones of the same period, where the

non ue altro che quatro uariera cioe, lungo, corto, alto con la punta e basso, i nasi concaui sono di tre sorti.

4

il Gobbo in mezo fra rette linee, il Gobbo in mezo fra curue linee conuesse, il Gobbo in mezo fra linee concaue,

5

1. Side by side profiles
   (1508-1510),
   Codex Atlanticus
   (fo. 635r).

2. Alexandrine artist,
   Gonzaga Cameo,
   (3th century BC),
   St. Petersburg,
   the Hermitage.

3. Francesco
   di Simone Ferrucci,
   Scipion
   (c. 1475),
   Paris, Louvre.

4. Profile of
   an ancient captain
   (1475-1480),
   London,
   British Museum.

5. Herculean profile
   of a warrior
   (c. 1508),
   Turin,
   Biblioteca Reale.

concept of human life is seen in relation to that of the earth. But Leonardo was not merely a natural philosopher, in the Aristotelian sense. He was also a poet, in the sense of being able to evoke the dreams and images of infancy. And so it may be that Freud was right in recognising in the *Mona Lisa* an idealised portrait of Leonardo's mother.

DRAWING

In the Uffizi *Adoration of the Magi* Leonardo followed a new procedure, later to be emulated by the Venetians. It consisted of drawing the composition directly on the surface to be painted, without the aid of a cartoon but developing an idea tried out in preliminary drawings of relatively small size.

In all of the paintings brought by Leonardo to a high degree of completion the drawing is always impeccable. When Vasari reported the episode of Leonardo's father presenting his son to Andrea del Verrocchio he wrote: «One day [Ser Piero] took some of his drawings [and so it was drawing that first opened the way to Leonardo] and brought them to Andrea del Verrocchio, who was a very good friend of his, and urgently begged him to say whether Leonardo would profit from studying design. Andrea was amazed when he saw Leonardo's extraordinary beginnings».

Leonardo's talent in drawing thus seems to date back to a period preceding his apprenticeship with Verrocchio, but of this time no trace has remained, no documentary evidence.

Leonardo's first known drawing is the famous landscape in the Uffizi Gallery, dated «the day of Saint Mary of the Snow, 5 August 1473». The valley of the Arno is seen in a bird's eye view from a point on Montalbano

1

2

3

4

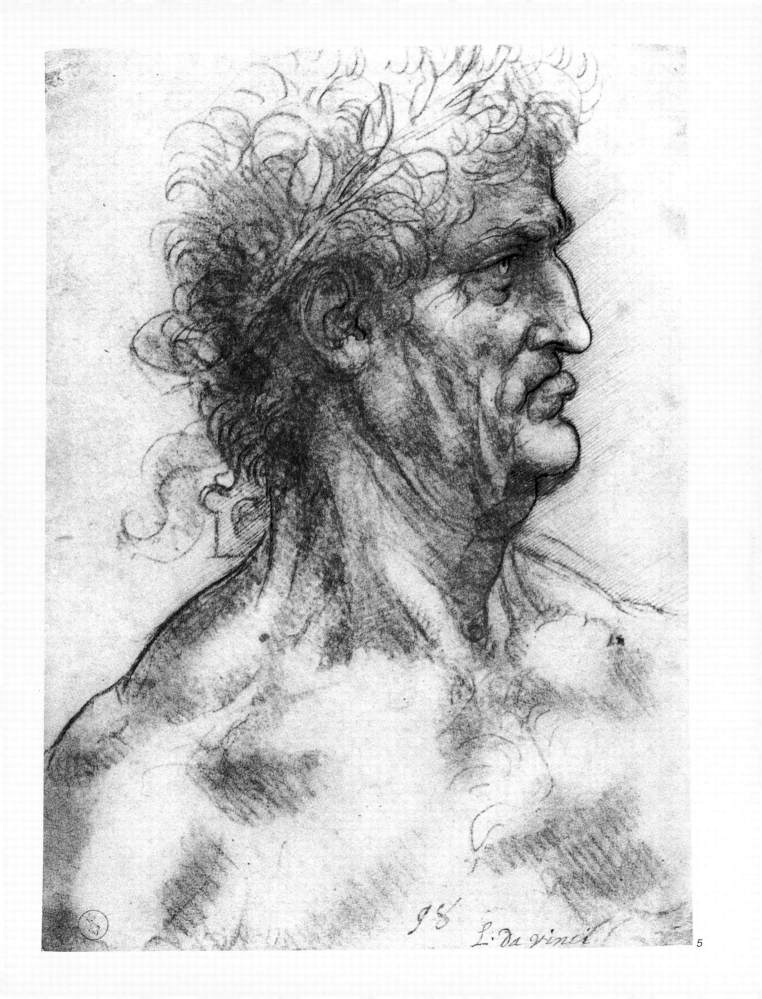

95 L. da vinci

5

1. *Study for
a standing cherub
(1506-1508)
detail,
Windsor,
Royal Library.*

2. *Studies of crabs
(c. 1480) detail,
Cologne,
Wallarf-Richartz
Museum.*
3. *Albrecht Dürer,
engraving
of the Accademia
Vinciana panels.*

4. *Engraving of the
Accademia Vinciana
(c. 1495),
Milan,
Biblioteca
Ambrosiana.*

5. *Decorative motifs
inspired by antiquity
on a folio of studies
for the* Adoration
*of the Magi
and other sketches
from life
(c. 1480),
Bayonne,
Musée Bonnat.*

1

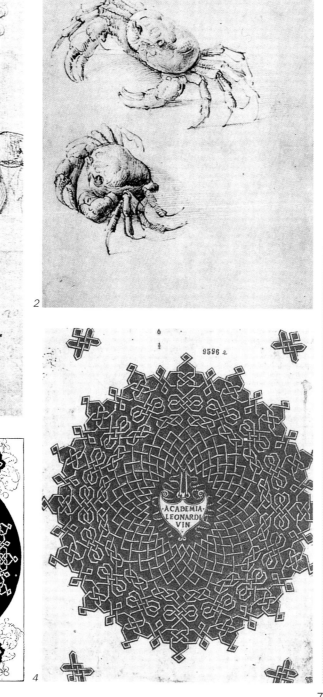

2

4

near Vinci. The drawing was done with the left hand, like all of Leonardo's known drawings. Since the artist was then twenty years old, it was not drawn before he moved to Florence. And in fact all of the drawings from Leonardo's so-called youthful period published up to now are later than 1473, including the one in the Morgan Library at New York recently acknowledged to be his.

The youthful drawings, especially the studies for the personages in the *Adoration of the Magi* (now dispersed among Florence, Venice, Hamburg, Cologne, Paris, Bayonne, London and Windsor) are distinguished by a melodic quality in the line which flows to embody a new sense of grace, still of Neo-platonic influence, as noted already by Leon Battista Alberti in the beauty of the women's faces; a grace fully expressed in the motion and postures of Leonardo's figures, which would be emulated by Raphael over thirty years later.

But the folios with the studies for the *Adoration* contain other things as well: curiosities, fantasies, whimsy. On the back of the folio with the Cologne drawing, for instance, are two crabs. On another folio, now at Bayonne, Leonardo drew two standing cherubs, one of whom has loaded an enormous crab on his shoulders. Leonardo's playfulness had begun to emerge, that special taste of his for the surprise effect, for new themes and motifs, often destined to go no further than the drawing, the first idea or conception, like a sudden joke. Playing on words taken from a vast repertoire of objects and figures, turning them into ideograms and rebus: this was the exuberant whimsicality that would cause Vasari to reproach him for his "divertissement", classifying among such even those masterpieces which are the

5

*1. Albrecht Dürer,
Perspectograph
(1525).*
*2. Portrait painted with
the perspectograph
(c. 1490),
Windsor,
Royal Library.*

*3. Portrait painted
with the
perspectograph
(c. 1495),
attributed by Adolfo
Venturi (1930)
to Leonardo.*

4. Studies for a Nativity
*(c. 1483),
New York,
Metropolitan
Museum.*
*5. Albrecht Dürer,
Perspectograph
(1525).*

*6. Bellows machine
for drawing up water
and man portraying
an armillary sphere
with a perspectograph
(c. 1480),
Codex Atlanticus
(fo. 5r).*

pages of the so-called Accademia Vinciana: six copper prints with variations on the theme of interwoven emblems.

Here Leonardo's drawing becomes a synthesis of the concept of creative, and thus cosmic, knowledge, manifested in the abstract language of geometry, appearing as symbol of law and order in nature and as inexhaustible stimulus to the imagination.

A node of this kind, albeit in the embryonic state and barely perceptible in a faint charcoal drawing, is already present on the back of Leonardo's first known drawing, the landscape from 1473. Clearer and more varied, the same nodes reappear on another youthful folio with studies of hydraulic technology in the Codex Atlanticus.

Alongside these nodes is the drawing of a perspectograph for the mechanical reproduction of objects (in this case an armillary sphere) or persons, a device based on the Albertian principle of the square or "graticule" as intersecting plane of the visual cone, which Leonardo codified in texts from about 1490 destined to the *Trattato della pittura.* There he described the two types of perspectograph which were to be made famous by Dürer's illustrations thirty-five years later. One of them has a graticule or glass on which the observed image is delineated, then to be transferred by tracing to a sheet of paper. In the other the graticule is replaced by a reticle, the same used to prepare the sheet of paper on which the painter draws the features of the figure observed through the sight: borderlines or profiles defined in the space divided into squares.

In the sheet of studies for a *Nativity* now in the Metropolitan Museum, where the infant St. John appears in the role of playmate to the Christ

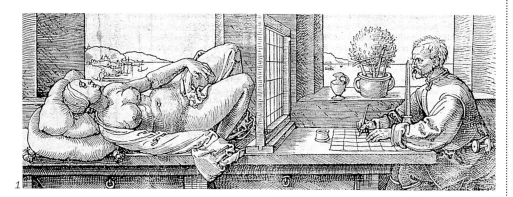

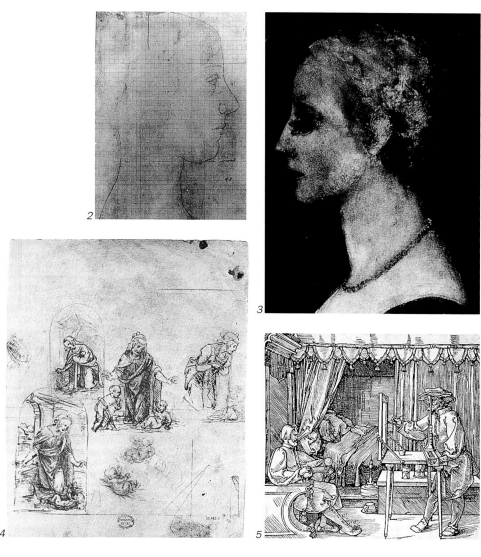

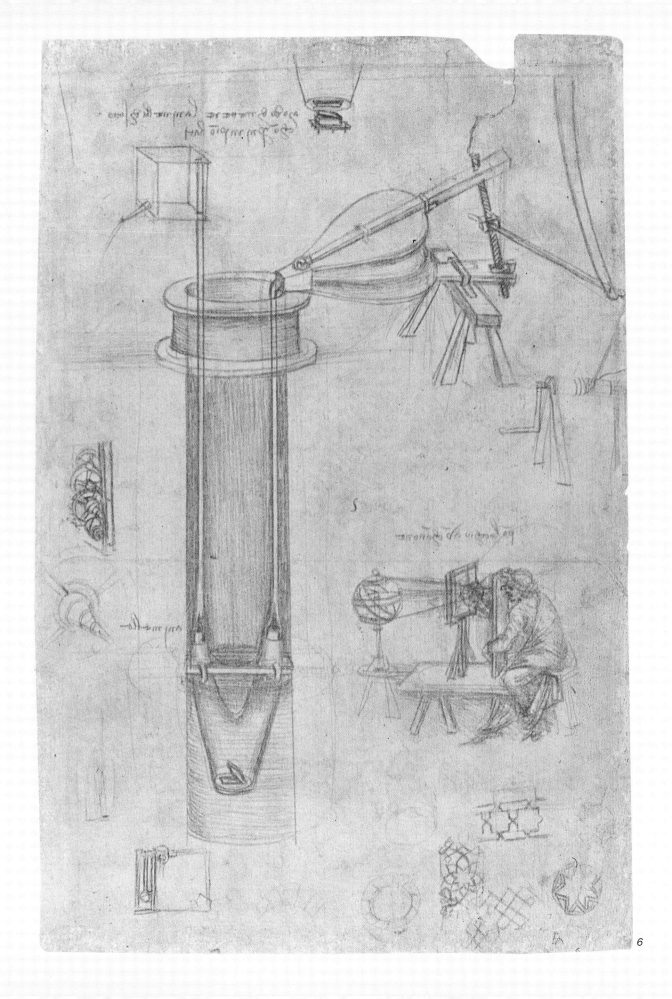

6

1. Homo Vitruvianus, *from Cesare Cesariano's edition of Vitruvius (Como 1521).*

2. Homo Vitruvianus as a Robot *from the dust jacket of the book by Mark E. Rosheim,* Robot Wrist Actuators *(New York 1989).*

3. *Geometric proportions applied to the human figure,* Windsor, Royal Library *(RL 19132r).*

4. *Homo Vitruvianus, study of proportions with the human figure inscribed in a circle and a square (c. 1490),* Venice, Gallerie dell'Accademia.

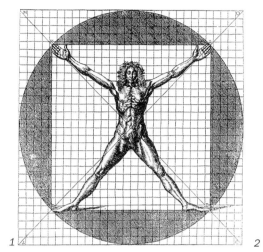

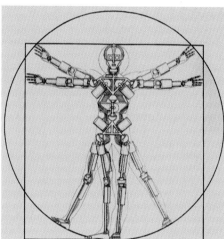

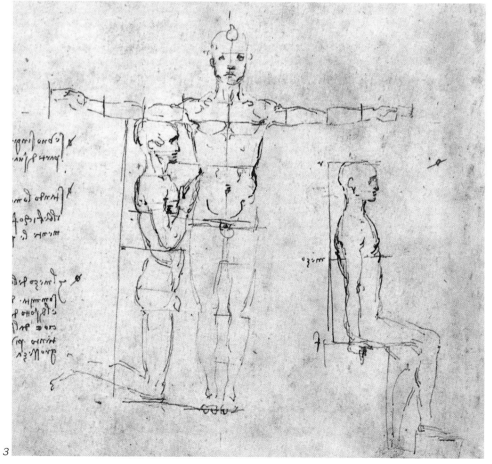

Child, the development of Leonardo's iconography and composition which was to lead to the Louvre *Virgin of the Rocks* can be observed. The head of the kneeling angel at the right can instead be studied in a famous drawing in Turin, in which a young woman is viewed from the shoulders, her bust seen in profile.

In this drawing many have recognised Cecilia Gallerani, the splendid *Lady of the Ermine*, a painting also conceived as a "shoulder" portrait, but from a different angle of perspective. In fact, starting from the early drawings of a woman's bust observed from various points of view Leonardo arrived, in the Turin study, at formulating a basic principle of "action motion", the motion that a figures makes "in itself", without changing position and with the implicit suggestion of a spiral process; motion which is the very germ of the "serpentine" characteristic of Michelangelo and the Mannerists, but which was in effect introduced by Leonardo with his studies for the kneeling *Leda* and the standing one (Rotterdam, Chatsworth and Windsor).

These developments emerged from 1503 to 1510 and beyond, when Leonardo's drawing became more emphatic, especially in the anatomical studies, with hatching that curves to follow the form, accentuating its sense of volume.

The final result shows marked characteristics of classic monumentality, attained through a process involving the studies for the apostles in the *Last Supper* and above all the figure of the Virgin in the *Madonna of the Yarn Winders*, studied in a powerful drawing now at Windsor, and that of *Saint Anne* in the London cartoon, and so on to the Louvre's enigmatic *St. John the Baptist*.

One of Leonardo's most famous

1. Anonymous,
Angel of the
Annunciation,
copy from Leonardo,
Basle,
Kunstmuseum.

2. Drawing
of whirlpools, detail,
Windsor,
Royal Library
(no. 12579r).

3. Study of dancers
(c. 1515),
drawing
recomposed
of two fragments,
Venice,
Gallerie
dell'Accademia.

4. Bacchus
(1511-1515),
Paris,
Louvre.

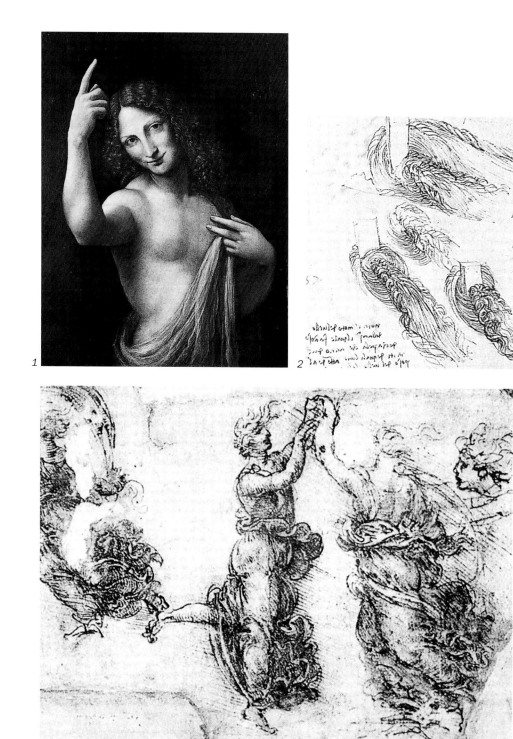

1

2

3

drawings, the so-called *Homo Vitru vianus* in Venice, illustrates the can on of human proportions that Vitru vius, the Roman architect of the 1 century BC, had postulated as basi for his architectural theory. In Vitru vius' text, transcribed by Leonardo i an Italian version, the human figure i inserted first in a circle and then in square, a procedure always followe in the illustrations to Vitruvius' trea tise, starting from the one edited b Fra Giocondo in 1511.

Twenty years earlier then, in 1490 the date of the Venice drawing, Leo nardo had already thought of using i as illustration, producing a visua synthesis of Vitruvius' demonstratio through the simultaneous perception of two different superimposed trans parent images, to suggest the possi bility of motion from one position t another. Yet one of Leonardo's figure is surprising. The nude man inscribe in the square is distinguished by a erect member and by long curly hai adorned with vine leaves. Now ther is nothing in Vitruvius' text to justify the presence of the erection. Leonar do's figure seems a young Bacchu with features resembling those of th angel of the *Annunciation*. It is only natural then to link this figure to drawing recently found in German in which the angel of the *Annuncia tion* is transformed into the demonia cal image of a young Bacchus with a erection, viewed foreshortened, lik his raised arm. This may be an indi rect confirmation of the suspecte metamorphosis of the Louvre *St. John the Baptist* into a Bacchus. It is in fac a drawing that for technique and styl can be dated at the same time as tha painting, around 1513-1515.

Moreover, on the back of the re found folio Leonardo has noted three words in Greek — "astrapen", "bron ten", "ceraunobolian" – taken from

4

1. Studies of lines of force in currents of «acqua panniculata» (1508) detail, Manuscript F.

2. Studies of fabric, probably military tents, uprooted by the wind (c. 1515), Codex Atlanticus.

3. Study for a Deluge *(c. 1515), Windsor, Royal Library.*

4. Study for a Deluge, *Windsor, Royal Library (no. 12380).*

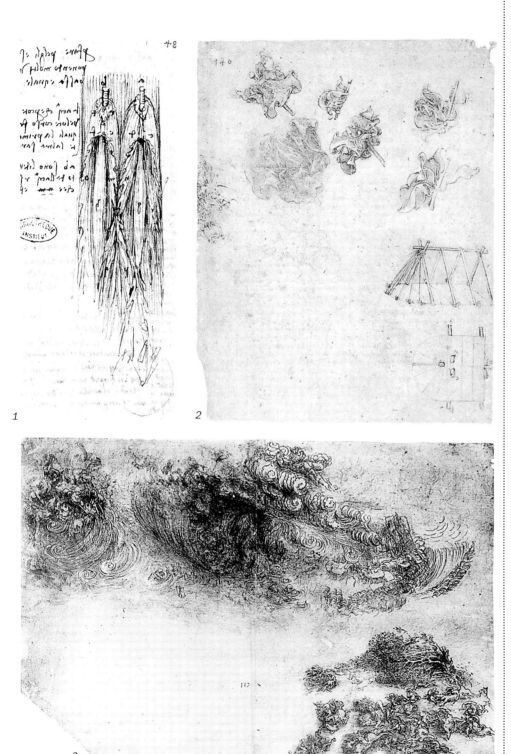

1

2

3

text by Pliny extolling Apelles' ability to paint what cannot be painted, atmospheric phenomena such as the flashes of lightening and thunderbolts indicated by the three words in Greek.

Leonardo himself, in a spirit of emulation, finally managed to portray such phenomena in about 1515 with the stupendous series of drawings of the *Deluge* in the Windsor collection and the Codex Atlanticus.

Dating from the same period are drawings on the theme of drapery already confronted by Leonardo at the very beginning. Fabric too could be caught in the wind, and the complexity of its motion had to be analysed, recorded and then codified like that of the elements themselves. From this come the enigmatic drawings on a folio in the Codex Atlanticus where only recently has it been possible to recognise the same objects depicted in the stormy sky of one of the Windsor drawings of the *Deluge*: military tents uprooted by the fury of the wind. Within this same context are the stupendous figures of dancers now in Venice and the so-called *Pointing Lady* of Windsor, where the theme is that of clothing whirled about by the wind.

THE PROBLEM OF THE SELF-PORTRAIT

Other important considerations are introduced by the theme of the self-portrait. The famous drawing in Turin, the best-known *Self-portrait* of Leonardo, remains stubbornly anchored to a date, 1512, consistent with the authority and wisdom emanating from an artist who has reached the age of sixty.

And yet dating at 1515, if not even later, cannot be excluded. Stylistic similarities to the so-called *Allegory of Fluvial Navigation* at Windsor, the

4

1. *Study of an old
   man seated
   (c. 1513) detail,
   Windsor,
   Royal Library.*

2. *Raphael,
   The School of Athens
   (1510)
   detail of Plato,
   Vatican City,
   Palazzi Vaticani,
   Stanza
   della Segnatura.*

3. *Allegory
   of navigation
   (c. 1516),
   Windsor,
   Royal Library.*

4. *Self-portrait
   (after 1515),
   Turin,
   Biblioteca Reale.*

1

2

3

one with the dog in the boat, also a red-chalk drawing and datable at that time, are obvious.

Turning then from style to iconography, the suspicion arises that the age represented could suggest dating during the French period, after 1517, when the sixty-five-year-old Leonardo appeared, to those who met him in October 1517, already «an old man over seventy».

For this reason it would be useful to ascertain whether the Turin folio is still as it was when Leonardo drew on it his self-portrait. The ratio between base and height suggests the elongated format of the folios he used in France. But the measurements are not the same, suggesting that the folio may have been trimmed at the sides enough to make the presence of the shoulders less conspicuous and to confer on the personage an erect position which in effect it did not have.

The venerable aspect would in fact be lacking if Leonardo appeared seated with his shoulders bowed like Raphael's *Julius II*.

In the well-known Windsor drawing (c. 1513) depicting an old man seated beside whirlpools of water, which has been thought to be a profile of Leonardo, the neck is in fact sunk between the shoulders.

The format used for the Turin drawing is larger than that of any other portrait drawn by Leonardo, except for the portrait of *Isabella d'Este* in the Louvre, which is however a cartoon perforated for transferral to a painting.

The large Oxford drawing of the so-called *Scaramaccia Captain of the Gypsies* belongs to the category of grotesques, and might also be a study for a painting (it is in fact perforated for transferral) or perhaps a drawing from 1515, when Leonardo was resid-

4

1. Adoration
   of the Magi
   (c. 1481) detail,
   Florence,
   Uffizi Gallery.

2. *James the Elder*
   (c. 1495),
   Windsor,
   Royal Library.

3. *Giorgio Vasari,*
   Portrait
   of Leonardo,
   from The Lives,
   1568 edition.

ing in the Vatican, of a court jester or juggler.

Some have seen a self-portrait in the Windsor study for the apostle James the Elder, in which the age represented seems that of a man about forty-five. The marked arch of the eyebrows, the prominent nose and cheekbones, the wide mouth with the well-modelled lips, could be viewed within a process of transformation that in twenty years would have led to the Turin self-portrait.

But in this process it is difficult if not impossible to insert the Windsor profile, of which the Ambrosiana possesses a copy, drawn by a pupil as a portrait of Leonardo, where the age is certainly not over fifty and the features seem more appropriate to the figure of a Saviour. All this has given rise to the perplexity, still unresolved, as to whether or not the Turin red-chalk drawing can be identified as a self-portrait of Leonardo.

Still another hypothesis has been advanced, that of the stereotype, in which the Turin drawing might be an idealised image, rather than a true self-portrait. Apart from the singular proposal by Hans Ost that the Turin drawing is a fake done by Giuseppe Bossi in the early 19th century, it has also been suggested, by Robert Payne for instance, that it should be recognised as a portrait of Leonardo's father drawn in about 1503.

Payne has remarked that the Turin drawing actually represents an old man over seventy, as was in fact Ser Piero da Vinci in the early 16th century, but the suggestion fails to take account of the fact that Leonardo himself appeared to have this same age to those who met him at Amboise in 1517.

In Milan Leonardo gathered around him pupils and follows who assimilated his style, interpreting it in their own works. A long-debated question is whether or not the Leonardo school should be considered a real academy modelled on the Neoplatonic one sponsored by Lorenzo de' Medici in Florence for the humanists and philosophers who gathered around Marsilio Ficino. Undoubtedly, it welcomed not only apprentices, as was still customary in the workshops of the time, but also affirmed masters who were

offered the chance to practice their profession within the framework of an important institution.

The school seems to have been most successful in producing portraits, where the intervention of Leonardo might even be limited to the concept or the initial idea alone. Among the painters in Accademia Vinciana were the brothers Evangelista and Ambrogio De Predis, Marco d'Oggiono, Antonio Boltraffio and Francesco Napolitano.

Worthy of special mention are Oggiono and Boltraffio, both of whom may have collaborated on the *Last Supper*, and considered up until recently the painters of one of Leonardo's most admired portraits, the

LEONARDO AND HIS SCHOOL

Above, from left: *Giovan Antonio Boltraffio*, Symbolic Portrait *(c. 1500), Florence, Uffizi Gallery; Marco d'Oggiono*, The Holy Children; *Giovan Antonio Boltraffio*, Portrait of Gerolamo Casio *(c. 1500), Milano, Pinacoteca di Brera.* Below, from left: *Giovan Antonio Boltraffio*,

Symbolic Portrait on the Theme of St. Sebastian *(c. 1500), Moscow, Puškin Fine Arts Museum; Giovan Antonio Boltraffio*, Portrait of a Woman *(c. 1500), Milan, Biblioteca Ambrosiana; Emblem of the* Achademia Leonardi Vinci *(1495), engraving, London, British Museum.*

Lady of the Ermine, attributed first to one, then to the other. In Oggiono's production (c. 1475 - c. 1530), abundant but poorly documented, the obvious influence of Leonardo is reinforced by reference to coeval Lombard sculpture.

Among his certain works are the signed polyptych in the museum at Blois, the altarpieces at Brera (*The three archangels*) and the *Madonna and Saints* of the Besate parish house near Abbiategrasso.

Of Antonio Boltraffio (Milan 1466/ 1467-1516) portraits in

particular are known, of clear Leonardesque imprint (even the Ambrosiana *Musician* was attributed to him for years), as well as the Portrait of *Gerolamo Casio* at Brera and innumerable portraits of women. His Madonnas reflecting, with elegant variations, the models of the master are highly popular.

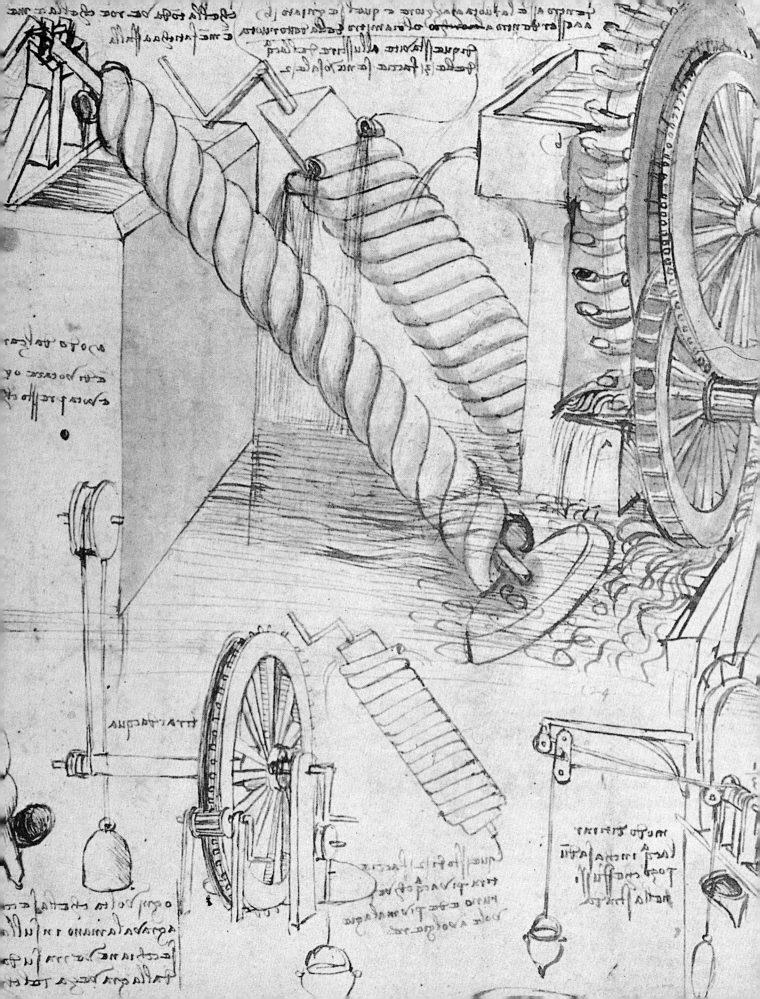

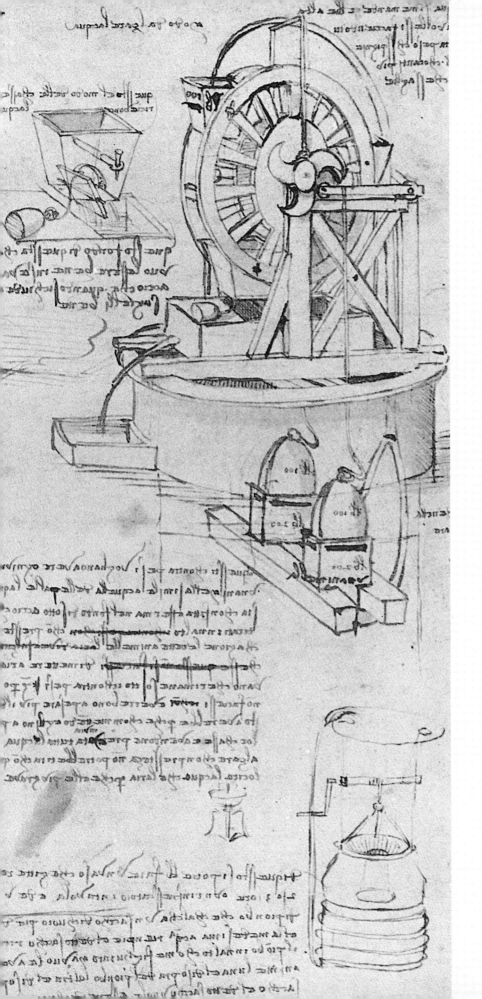

The codices

For almost all his life Leonardo filled codices and notebooks with drawings and writings, recording not only his most complex, profound thoughts but also curiosities, personal facts, and idiosyncrasies. The vicissitudes of Leonardo's codices are as intricate and complicated as the plot of a spy story, with personages contending the precious treasure in Europe and recently in America as well, and with scholars as committed to reconstructing their history as detectives hot on the trail of a geographically scattered terrain, possessing only a handful of documents to be compared and integrated with the innumeable folios already hard to decipher and jumbled in wild confusion by generations of different owners.

1. Two types of adjustable-opening compass, mortar-piece and mechanical parts (1493-1494), Manuscript H (ff. 108v and 109r).

2. Study of plants (c. 1506), Windsor, Royal Library.

3. Original binding of Manuscript C (17th century).

4. Studies of decorative motifs and of proportions of the head of a dog (1497-1498), Manuscript I (ff. 47v and 48r).

Upon the death of Leonardo in 1519 at Amboise, Francesco Melzi, the faithful disciple and friend of his last years, inherited all of the manuscripts written by his master. He brought them back to Italy where they were conserved and utilised (for example in extending the *Trattato della pittura*) until he too died in 1570 at his villa in Vaprio d'Adda near Milan.

After the death of Melzi there was a first dispersion of Leonardo's manuscripts in which Madrid became, at the turn of the 16th century, the place where most of the codices were concentrated. Here Pompeo Leoni, sculptor to the Spanish court, had managed to collect, it seems, up to fifty manuscripts and about two thousand scattered folios: an impressive collection to which were to be added the 283 folios (Codex Arundel) probably acquired in Spain by the Englishman Lord Arundel and the two codices recently (1966) rediscovered in the Biblioteca Nacional of Madrid.

At the death of Leoni, his heirs decided to sell his collection, and Leonardo's codices came back to Italy, again to Milan, purchased first in 1632 by Count Galeazzo Arconati, who in 1637 donated to the Biblioteca Ambrosiana the Codex Atlanticus and almost all of the Leonardo manuscripts now in Paris, at the Institut de France (Manuscripts A-M).

In about 1630 other manuscripts left for England, again from Madrid, and again from the Leoni inheritance: the above-mentioned Codex Arundel (now at the British Museum in London) as well as the book of 234 folios (Windsor collection) with extraordinary drawings of anatomy, figures, animals, and landscapes which then passed from the hands of the English lord to those of the royal family, which kept it in the library of Windsor Castle. Only

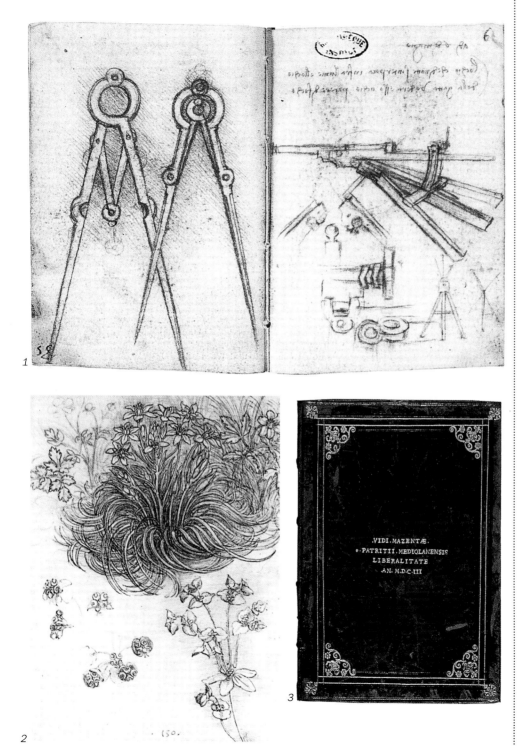

.VIDI.MAZENTÆ.
.PATRITII.MEDIOLANENSIS
LIBERALITATE
.AN. M.D.C.III

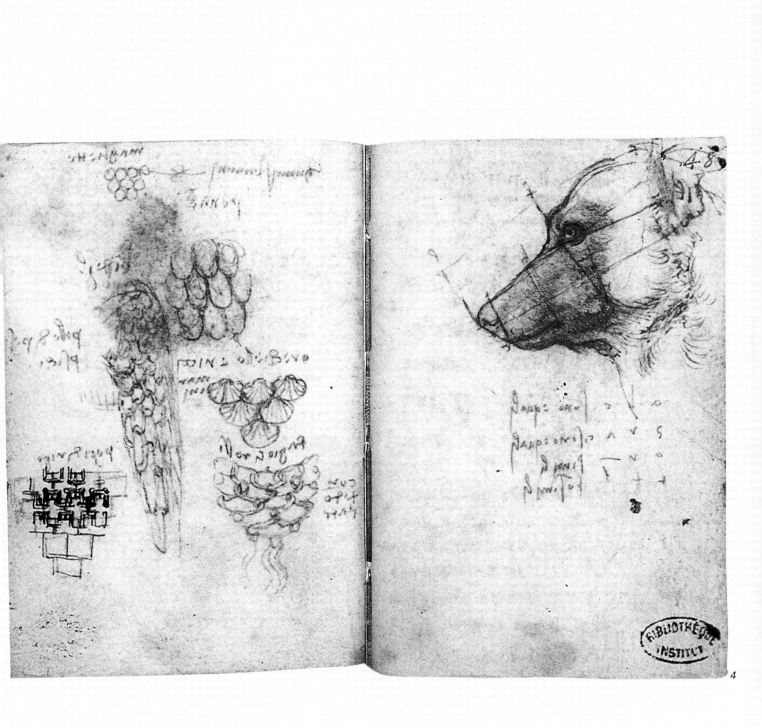

4

1. Study of
mechanisms and
for a hygrometer
(c. 1480),
Codex Atlanticus.

2. Drawing
of a machine
for draining canals
(1513-1514),
Manuscript E
(fo. 75v).

3. Study of a
centrifugal pump
for draining swamps
(c. 1508),
Manuscript F
(fo. 15r).

4. Volcanic explosion
(c. 1517),
Windsor,
Royal Library.

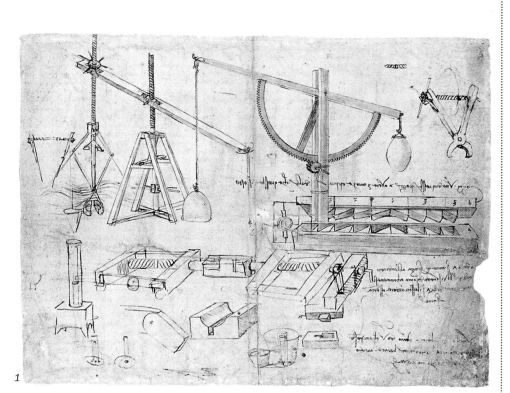

1

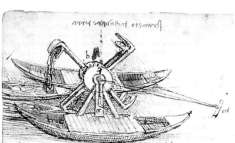

2

3

since 1873 has information been available on the three codices that reached England, in what way is not known, to be purchased by John Forster who then donated them to the Victoria and Albert Museum in London.

The geographical location of the codices, thus distributed in the mid-17th century between Milan, Madrid and London, was abruptly disarranged in 1795 when General Napoleon Bonaparte, in a gesture that was already "imperial", ordered all of Leonardo's codices to be transferred from the Biblioteca Ambrosiana in Milan to Paris.

At the end of the 18th century the French capital thus suddenly became one of the outstanding sites in the geography of the codices, although the Codex Atlanticus (and it alone) was returned to Milan after the Congress of Vienna in 1815.

In the mid-19th century the so-called "Guglielmo Libri case" occurred. This naturalised Frenchman, professor of mathematics and illustrious historian of science who had risen fast in his career as director of French libraries, during an official inspection at the Institut de France removed a number of sheets from Leonardo's manuscripts, including even the small Codex on the Flight of Birds.

Libri then fled to England where he rearranged the folios he had removed in "codices" which he managed to sell to Lord Ashburnham, from whom they were later purchased again by France.

More straightforward is the path of the Leonardo codex which arrived in the hands of the 16th century sculptor Guglielmo della Porta by other ways than those of the Melzi heredity, and was then bought by the painter Giuseppe Ghezzi. The latter sold it in 1717 to the future Count of Leicester, who was travelling in Italy at the time.

4

1. *Anonymous 16th century, drawings of machines copied from folios by Leonardo, in part lost (c. 1530), Florence, Uffizi Gallery, Gabinetto dei disegni e delle stampe.*

2. *Drawing of a mortar (c. 1485), Codex Atlanticus (fo. 59v).*

3. *Archimedes screws and pumps to draw up water (c. 1480), Codex Atlanticus (fo. 26v).*

4. *System of defence and studies of horses for the Battle of Anghiari (c. 1504), Codex Atlanticus (fo. 72r).*

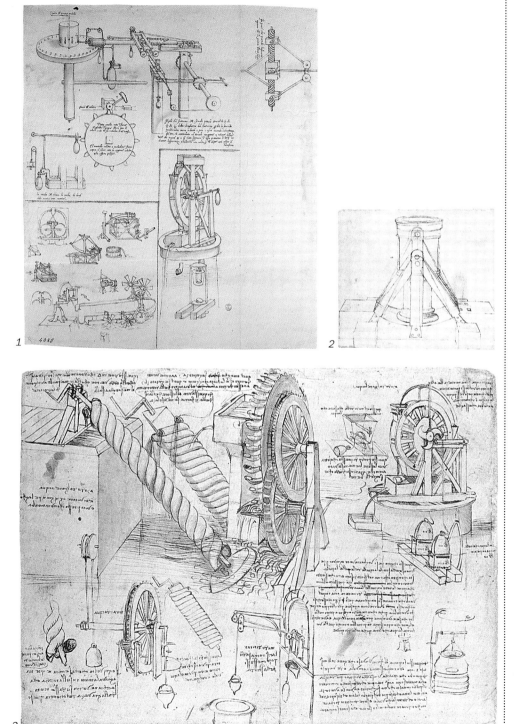

Known as the Codex Leicester for the next two hundred and sixty years, this manuscript has made the headlines in recent years for the sensational auctions in which it has changed hands twice, bringing it to the United States. Purchased in 1980 by the oil millionaire Armand Hammer (who gave it the name by which it is now known), and then bought in 1994 by Bill Gates, the computer magnate, it is the only codex that has remained private property.

THE CODEX ATLANTICUS

The Codex Atlanticus (Milan, Biblioteca Ambrosiana), with its original 16th century binding, is, with its 401 pages, the largest and most extraordinary collection of Leonardian folios in existence. The name derives from the large format (65x44 cm), of the Atlas type, of its pages. Although it may appear to be a real codex, a book arranged by its author to be filled with drawings and notes, it is in reality a miscellaneous collection of folios and fragments collected in single volume by the sculptor Pompeo Leoni. A debatable attempt at restoration was made in the 1960s-70s.

The material in the Codex Atlanticus encompasses Leonardo's entire career, for a period of over 40 years, from 1478 when he was twenty-six to his death in 1519. It contains the richest documentation on his contributions to the sciences of mechanics and mathematics, to astronomy, physical geography, botany, chemistry and anatomy; but also a record of his thoughts expressed in fables, apologies, and philosophical meditation.

Furthermore, there are notes on the theoretical and practical aspects of painting and sculpture, on optics, perspective, the theory of light and shadow, down to the materials used by the artist, as well as numerous studies

4

1. Original binding
of the Windsor
collection
(16th century)
in red leather with
decorations in gold,
48x35 cm,
Windsor,
Royal Library.

2. Draped torso
of an old man
(c. 1489) detail,
"Landscapes",
Windsor,
Royal Library
(fo. 1r).

3. Study of two plants
for the Leda
(c. 1508-1510),
"Landscapes",
Windsor,
Royal Library
(fo. 23r).

4. Study of muscles
of the trunk
and of the thigh
(1510),
Windsor,
Royal Library.

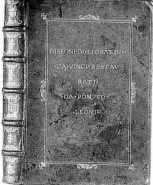

such as those for the *Adoration of the Magi*, the *Leda*, the *Battle of Anghiari*, and projects for the monuments to Francesco Sforza and Gian Giacomo Trivulzio, and even for the construction of automatons.

WINDSOR COLLECTION

Everything indicates that this volume – owned by the British royal family since 1690 – is the book of 234 folios listed in the inventory of the property of Leoni compiled in 1609 (with addenda in 1613), a book that up to 1630 was in the possession of Lord Arundel who had bought it in Spain from Leoni's heirs.

It is a miscellaneous collection with the original binding. On its pages Leoni mounted about six hundred drawings executed by Leonardo between 1478 and 1518, of varying format and subject matter.

In the late 19th century the work of disassembly was begun, concluding in 1994 with the individual folios placed between two sheets of perspex, an operation which ensures better viewing and conservation, as well as the arrangement of the folios by subject and chronology according to the cataloguing scheme adopted by Carlo Pedretti in publishing them in facsimile.

The codex opens with the section "Anatomy", the most conspicuous nucleus (about two hundred drawings) fruit of thirty years of studies conducted by Leonardo directly on the human body through the dissection of over thirty cadavers.

This is followed by "Landscapes" among them the extraordinary *Deluges*, then by "Horses and Other Animals" in which appear studies for the youthful Adorations, for the monuments to Sforza and to Trivulzio and for the *Battle of Anghiari*.

The section "Figures, Profiles, Caricatures" includes studies for the *Vir-*

1. *Study of stage
   sets for Poliziano's
   Orpheus
   (c. 1506-1508),
   Codex Arundel
   (ff. 231v and 224r).*

2. *Studies of shadows
   (1510-1515),
   Codex Arundel
   (ff. 246v and 243r).*

3. *Study of floater
   with breathing tubes
   for a diver
   (1508),
   Codex Arundel
   (fo. 24v).*

gin of the Rocks* and the beautiful nu
cleus of fifteen folios for the *Las
Supper.*

Lastly, the "Miscellaneous Papers"
contain various material including re
bus, emblems and allegories.

CODEX ARUNDEL

This codex too (London, British Mu
seum) is in reality a miscellaneou
collection, not of scattered sheets o
fragments, but of booklets, with a to
tal of 283 folios of various forma
mainly 21x15 cm. The history of thi
manuscript is obscure, especially i
the early stages. It is not, in fact, liste
among the volumes possessed b
Leoni, although it is highly probabl
that Lord Arundel had purchased it i
Spain in the 1630s. Certainly in hi
possession in 1642, the codex was do
nated by Lord Arundel's heirs to th
Royal Society of London in 1666; the
in 1831-1832, it was transferred to th
British Museum.

Mathematics is the dominant them
of this manuscript. From some note
on expenses and reminders, often dat
ed, the chronology of the folios can b
determined: the first 30 are from 150
(in realty, 1509), while the others dat
from 1478 to 1518.

On some of the individual folio
there are drawings of ingenious ob
jects, such as the device with mask
and tubes for breathing underwater.

FRENCH MANUSCRIPTS

Now in Paris, at the Institut de France
are twelve codices which differ i
format, number of pages, binding
chronology and content. In 1795 Na
poleon Bonaparte had them brough
here from the Biblioteca Ambrosian
in Milan. The indications A-M, fro
the end of the 18th century, were as
signed by the Abbot Giovan Battist
Venturi. Of small, even pocket-book
size, these little books with thei

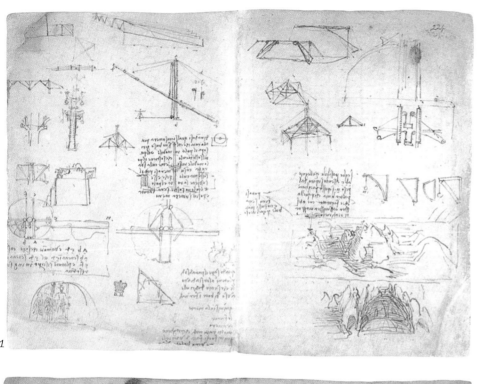

1

2

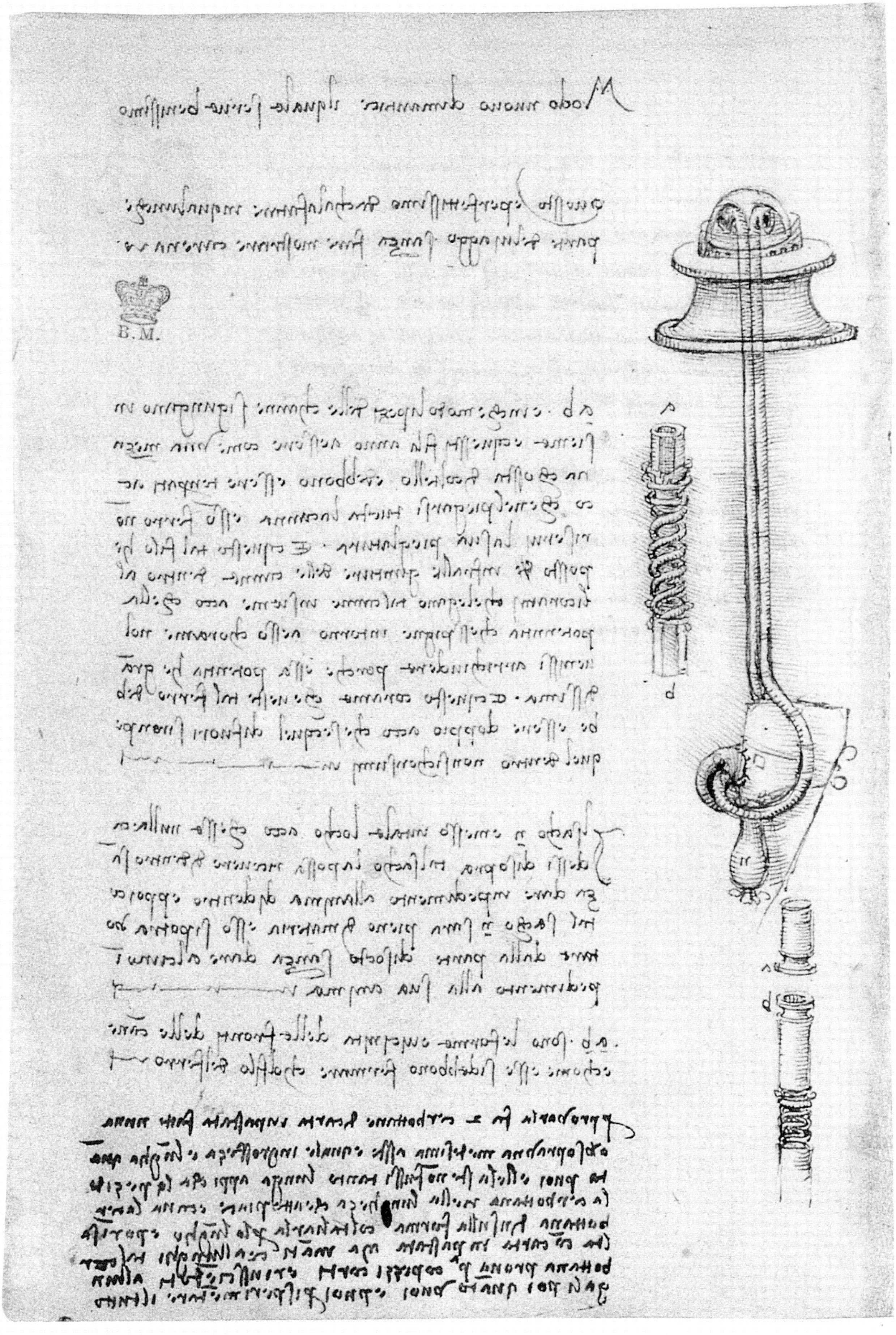
B.M.

1. Manuscript K,
Paris,
Institut de France.
2. Rays of light
through an angular
opening
(1490-1491),
Manuscript C
(fo. 10v).

3. Manuscript I, Paris,
Institut de France.
4. Machinery
for manufacturing
concave mirrors;
study on shearing
power with
mathematical
calculations
(c. 1515),

Manuscript G
(ff. 83v and 84r).
5. Clockwork for
planetary clocks
(c. 1498),
Manuscript L
(fo. 92v).
6. Balanced scales
and notes; studies
of comparative

anatomy
(1506-1507),
Manuscript K
(ff. 110r and 109v).
7. Coloured fruits
and vegetables on
a large ink-spot
(1487-1489),
Manuscript B
(fo. 2r).

drawings and notes conserve the form and the original characteristics of Leonardo's compiling, including the habit of beginning from the back of the book and proceeding toward the front (here it should be recalled that Leonardo was left-handed and that he wrote from right to left) and the frequent upside-down sheets. Of the twelve codices, Manuscript A (1490-1492) and Manuscript B (the oldest known of Leonardo's codices, dating from 1487-1489) were involved in the theft by Guglielmo Libri. Integral parts of them were the so-called Ashburnham codices 2038 and 2037 (put together by Libri of the sheets he had stolen, sold by him to Lord Ashburnham and then returned to the Institut de France in 1891).

In Manuscript B appears a series of futuristic drawings of flying machines, the submarine, and even an "aerial screw", a forerunner of the modern helicopter. Manuscript E is important (a late codex, containing notes from 1513-1514), from which Libri also robbed the last booklet, which was to be lost. The main section deals with mechanical physics, to which Leonardo made a determinant contribution. Manuscript F (1508), where the theme of water plays a major role, is one of the notebooks which has come down to us practically intact from the time of Leonardo. In Manuscript L (1497-1504) are notes on the *Last Supper*. Manuscript M (1499-1500) testifies to an important moment in the life of Leonardo, when he began to study some of the great classical authors, such as Euclid, whose lesson was to decidedly influence his observations on geometry, a significant subject in this codex.

CODICES FORSTER

These are three small codices (London, Victoria and Albert Museum), of

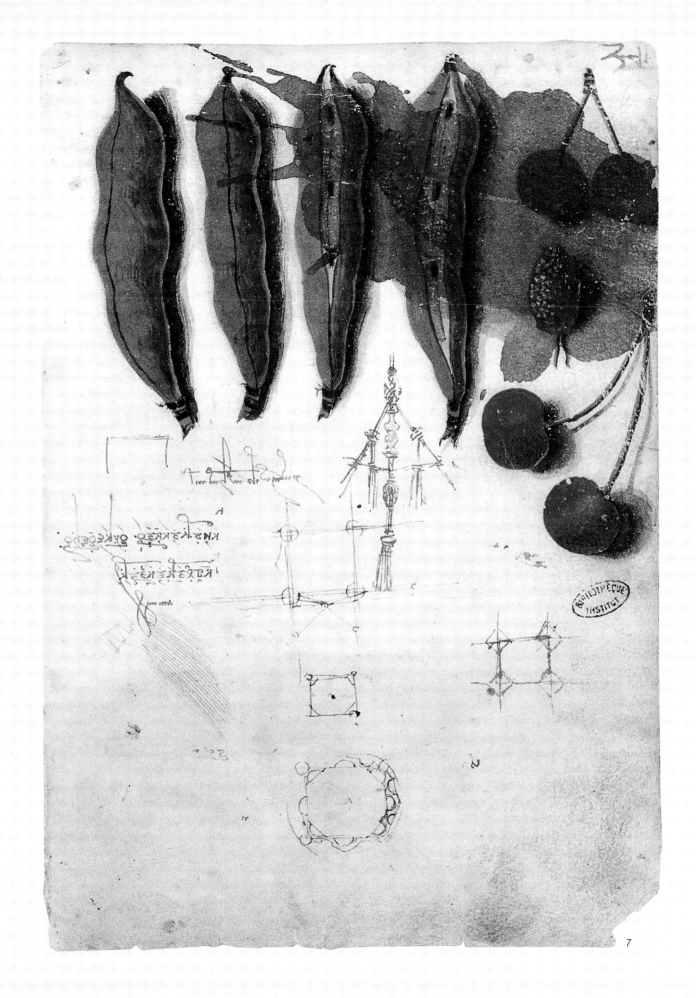

7

1. *Geometrical figure; proportional compass and its nutscrew (1505), Codex Forster I (fo. 4r).*

2. *Geometrical figures: dodecahedron and pyramid with pentagonal base (1505), Codex Forster I (fo. 7r).*

3. *Drawings of device for rotating wing (c. 1505), Codex on the Flight of Birds (ff. 16v and 17r).*

4. *Birds exploiting currents of air for their spiralling flight (c. 1505), Codex on the Flight of Birds (fo. 8r).*

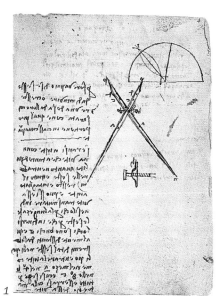

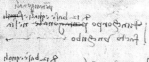

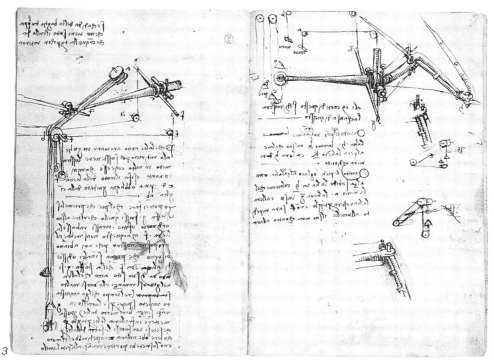

the pocket notebook type, which differ greatly in the subjects dealt with (geometry, hydraulic engineering, physics, but also literary questions, notes on the *Last Supper*, architectural projects, and practical notes of various kinds) as well as in dating (a span of time ranging from 1487 to 1505).

The three manuscripts met the common fate of passing from the ownership of Leoni to that of Lytton, then to be inherited by John Forster who bequeathed them to the London museum at his death in 1876.

CODEX ON THE FLIGHT OF BIRDS

Of small size (Turin, Biblioteca Reale; 21x15 cm), this codex formed part of Manuscript B from which, as previously mentioned, it was removed by Guglielmo Libri, who then dismembered it, selling five folios in England. The rest of the codex, now only thirteen folios, was purchased in 1867 by Count Giacomo Manzoni di Lugo. His heirs then sold it to the Russian Prince Theodore Sabachnikoff, who published the first printed edition after having acquired one of the five missing folios.

In 1893 Sabachnikoff donated the manuscript to the Savoia family. Placed in the Biblioteca Reale at Turin, it was completed with the four missing pages in the years between 1903 and 1920 and bound in 1967. As indicated by the name of the manuscript it consists mainly of studies on the flight of birds linked to attempts at building a flying machine.

The date 1505 appearing in the codex specifies its chronology, also in relation to the design of the flying machine. First conceived with beating winds, moved by the energy of human muscles, by this date it was instead designed as a kind of glider capable of exploiting currents of air.

1. Note on historical burning of the library at Alexandria; caricatures of heads; ironic verse on Petrarch (1487-1490), Codex Trivulziano (fo. 1v).

2. Clockwork mechanism (c. 1495-1499), Codex Madrid I (fo. 27v).

3. Clock spring and device for automatic release of loads; set of linked chains (c. 1495-1499), Codex Madrid I (ff. 9v and 10r).

4. Drawings for clockwork mechanisms and notes (c. 1495-1499), Codex Madrid I (ff. 13v and 14r).

1

2

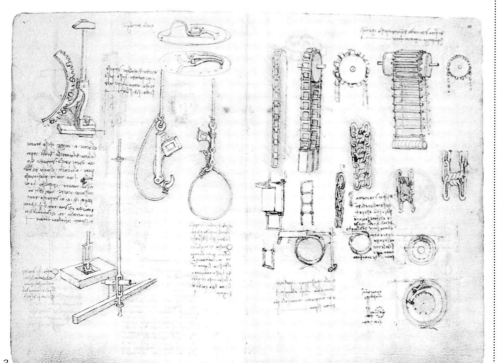

3

CODEX TRIVULZIANO

This codex, of format approximately 20.5x14 cm (Milan, Biblioteca del Castello Sforzesco Library) – originally consisting of 62 folios, several of which are missing today – was marked by Francesco Melzi with the letter F. Owned by Leoni and then by Arconati, it is described in the act of donation to the Biblioteca Ambrosiana (1637) but must have been taken back by Arconati in exchange for the volume then known as Manuscript D. News of this codex was then lost until it reappeared again in the possession of Gaetano Caccia, who gave it to Prince Trivulzio in 1750. With the Trivulziano collection it entered the Biblioteca del Castello Sforzesco in 1935. Bound with some of the booklets upside-down, its pages have been renumbered in red ink to avoid confusion in the order of the sheets. Among the oldest known manuscripts by Leonardo, it dates from the years 1487-1490.

CODICES MADRID

This is the name given to the two volumes found astonishingly – and by chance – in the Biblioteca Nacional of Madrid in 1966 and published in facsimile in 1973. It now seems certain that these are the two books possessed by Don Juan Espina, who probably received them through the Leoni heredity.

At the death of Espina the two volumes seem to have passed to the Spanish Crown and then to the Royal Library where they were catalogued for the first time in the inventory of 1831-1833. But in moving them (1830) along with other manuscripts from the palace to the Royal Library, an error was made in transcribing the designations, which blocked all attempts at finding them again until 1966.

In Codex Madrid II (dating for the most part from 1503-1505) there are

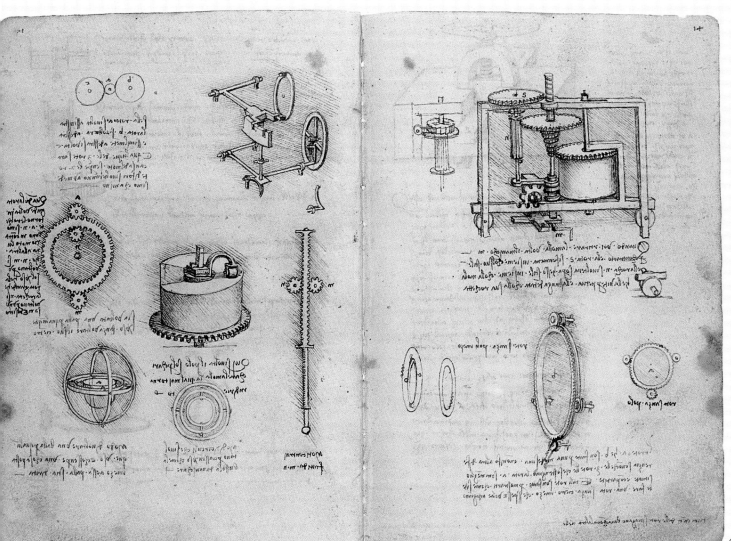

4

1. Study for the casting of the equestrian monument to Francesco Sforza (c. 1493) detail, Codex Madrid II (fo. 149r).

2. Antique binding of Codex Hammer (1720-1730).

3. Page of notes on the Moon; drawings and notes on lighting of the Sun, the Earth, the Moon (1506-1508), Codex Hammer (ff. 36v and 1r).

4. Siphons for studies on communicating vessels (c. 1506-1508) detail, Codex Hammer (fo. 34v).

5. Studies of "mechanical elements" (levers and springs) (c. 1497) detail, Codex Madrid I (fo. 44v-45r).

very important notes on the *Battle of Anghiari* and on perspective, which were used by Melzi in compiling the *Libro di pittura*. The manuscript also contains an inventory of books, of fundamental importance for defining "Leonardo's library".

CODEX HAMMER

Now at Seattle, in the Bill Gates collection, this is a group of 18 double sheets (thus 36 folios with recto and versus, having an average size of 29x 22 cm) which Leonardo compiled in pen and ink from 1506 to 1508, with additions made up to 1510, working on one dual sheet a time, each of which was then placed inside the others as in a book, but making of it a kind of mobile repertoire, open to reconsideration and revision. It is probable however that it was Leonardo himself who decided to have the folios sewn together to make a book, so that the manuscript can rightly be called a codex. After having been bought by Armand Hammer (1980), the codex was dismembered and now consists of loose sheets, as when Leonardo compiled it.

In 1994 it was purchased by Bill Gates, and has thus remained in the United States. The predominant theme of this manuscript is that of studies on water, illustrated by fascinating drawings of currents, waterfalls and whirlpools.

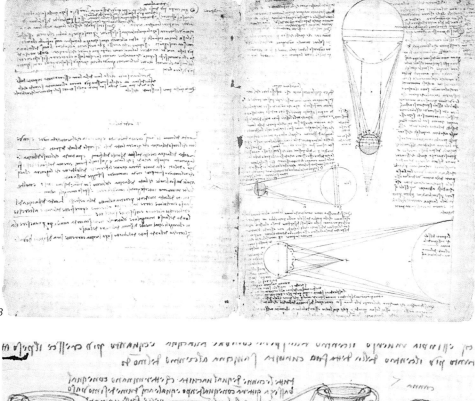

1

2

3

4

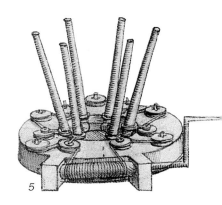

5

The study of Leonardo through his manuscripts has taken on the aspect of international co-operation, ensuring its continuity and effectiveness. The research organisations involved have developed around specialised libraries, such as the Biblioteca Leonardiana of Vinci, which is the oldest (founded in 1898), the Raccolta Vinciana of Milan (1905 wich edit since then the homonymous year-book), the Elmer Belt Library of Vinciana, donated by the founder to the University of California at Los Angeles in 1961 and since then incremented by Carlo Pedretti as professor and researcher. Pedretti has also established at the same university a Chair of Leonardo Studies unique the world over, made possible by the sponsorship of Armand Hammer, also responsible for the institution, in 1985, of the Hammer Center of Vincian Studies at the same university. Directed by Pedretti from the start, the Center carries out a program of academic and editorial activities and exhibitions (also in collaboration with the

LEONARDIAN INSTITUTIONS THROUGHOUT WORLD

The "villa" of Castel Vitoni, Italian headquarters of the Pedretti Foundation for Leonardo Studies. Below, from left: Elmer Belt, founder of the Elmer Belt Library

of Vinciana at Los Angeles; the bulletin of the Brescia Center for Leonardian Research; The Yearbook of the Hammer Center at Los Angeles.

programs of the local university, and maintaining contact with scholars all over the world.

Seminars, conferences and other academic activities have been favoured by the generous bequest of André Corbeau, including his vast Vincian library, to the University of Caen in Lower Normandy, France. Similar objectives are pursued by the Leonardo da Vinci Society at London, which has been active for some years under the guidance of Martin Kemp of the University of Oxford, with the periodic publication of a "Newsletter for Leonardisti".

An important Florence-based organisation is the Fondazione Leonardo da Vinci, which supports the activity of the Giunti publishing house as concerns the programs of the National Edition of Manuscripts and Drawings of Leonardo da Vinci, in particular with fellowships managed by the Museum and Institute of History of Science in the same city. The Vinciana Commission for the National Edition of the Works of Leonardo, a ministerial organisation founded in 1902,

Museo Ideale di Vinci, founded and directed by Alessandro Vezzosi) and publishes the yearbook "Achademia Leonardi Vinci" (Giunti). The Italian headquarters of the Hammer Center is lo-

cated at the Faculty of Philosophy of the University of Urbino.

Carlo Pedretti has also founded, again at Los Angeles but with a European base in his villa of Castel Vitoni at Lamporecchio above Vinci, the Foundation that carries out on his behalf an ambitious program of collaboration with cultural institutes in Italy and other European nations as well as the Near East, with Israeli universities in particular.

Already in 1977, at Brescia, another Leonardo expert, Nando De Toni, had founded a Center for Leonardian Research with the quarterly publication of a bulletin of bibliographical updating, repertoires and special contributions to the study of Leonardo's manuscripts and drawings,

and to their sources in particular. The activity of the Brescia Institute was then concentrated on the organisation of exhibitions and annual symposiums, also within the context of the

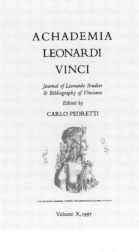

has recently assumed the function of research institute as well, promoting special projects aimed at producing working tools such as indexes, glossaries, repertoires and bibliographies.

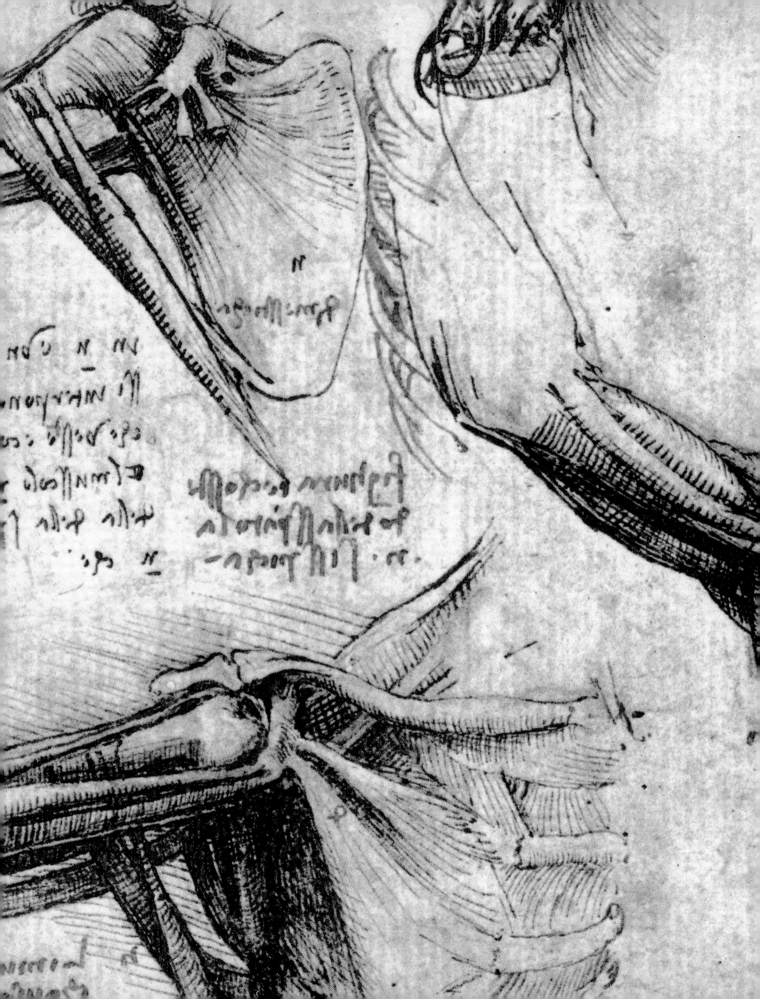

Anatomy

The corpus of Leonardo's anatomical drawings, composed of approximately two hundred folios, is kept in the Royal Library at Windsor. They are fascinating, intensely interesting drawings showing a superb balance between art and science. Leonardo dedicated himself to observation of the human body with a commitment so extraordinary as to arouse the admiration of his contemporaries. This is expressed in the words of Antonio De Beatis who in 1517 accompanied the Cardinal of Aragon on a visit to the studio of the now elderly Leonardo in France: «This gentleman has compiled a treatise on anatomy, with the demonstration in painting [...] in a way that has never yet been done by any other person. All of which we have seen with our eyes and he said that he has already dissected more than thirty bodies, both men and women of all ages».

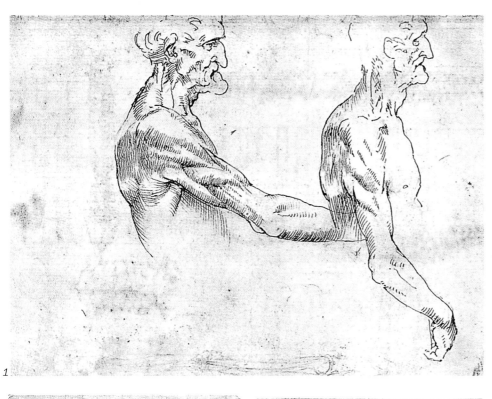

1

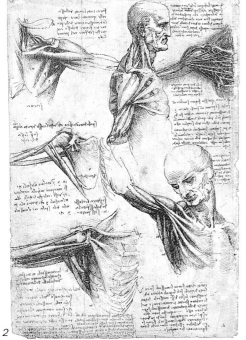

2

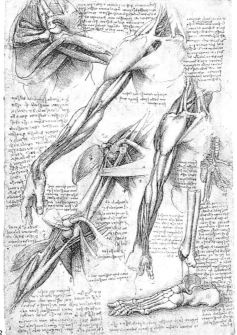

3

Up to the winter of 1507-1508 Leonardo did not practice dissection in any systematic way. At this time he had the opportunity of studying anatomy directly on the corpse of an old man in the hospital of Santa Maria Nuova in Florence, as he recalls in a famous note: «This old man, a few hours before his death, told me he was over a hundred years old, and that he felt no illness in his person apart from a certain weakness, and so sitting on a bed in the Hospital of Santa Maria Nova in Florence, with no other movement or any sign of accident, he passed out of this life. And I practised anatomy on him, to see what was the cause of such a gentle death [...], the which anatomy I performed very diligently and easily, as the old man had no fat or humours in him, which make it difficult to recognise the parts».

This experience, based on the direct observation of a cadaver rather than on acquired medical knowledge, was central to Leonardo's renewed anatomical interest. It was followed by the years of his stay in Lombardy (1510-1511) where he met and exchanged information with Marcantonio della Torre, a young but already renowned physician-anatomist in Pavia. Lastly, it is known that Leonardo conducted anatomical studies in Rome, between 1514 and 1515, in the Hospital of Santo Spirito, studies which were broken off due to an accusation of witchcraft resulting from the denouncement of his German assistant. The results of this decade of studies, while not decisive to the progress of medical science, were extraordinary in the field of anatomical illustration, which had been rough and crude before.

Leonardo decided to compile an

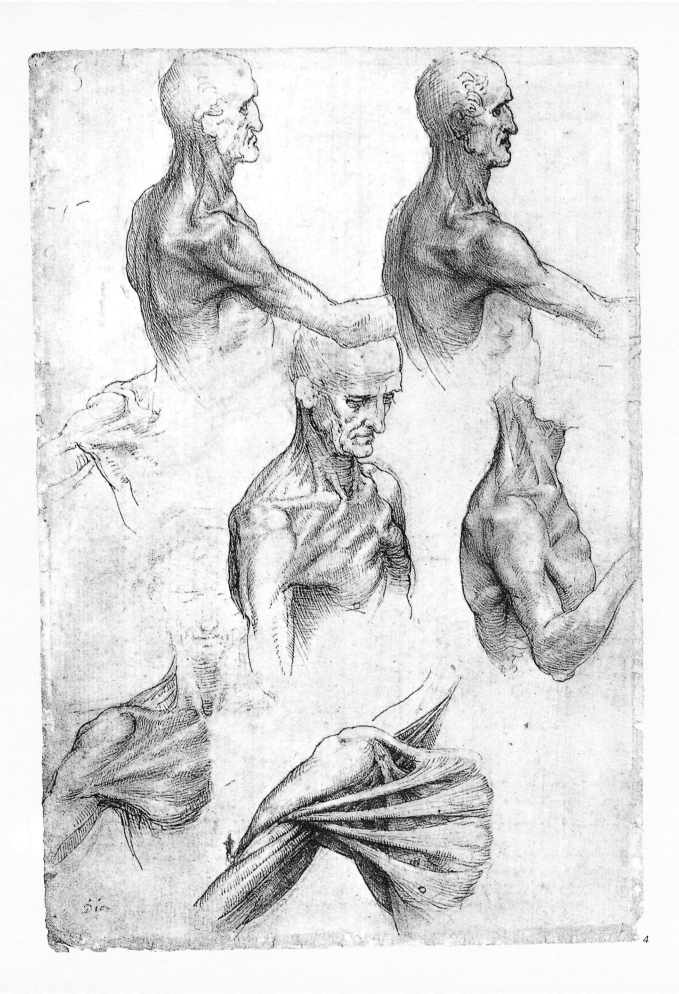

4

1. Anatomical figure
depicting heart,
lungs and main
arteries
(1490-1500),
Windsor,
Royal Library
(RL 12597r;
K/P 36r).
2. Male genital

organs, bladder
and urinary
and seminal canal;
pig's lung
(1508-1509),
Windsor,
Royal Library
(RL 19098v;
K/P 106v).

3. Muscles of the arm

in rotation; tongue,
throat and uvula
(c. 1508-1510),
Windsor,
Royal Library
(RL 19005v;
K/P 141v).
4. Superficial veins
detail,
Windsor,

Royal Library
(RL 19027r;
K/P 69r).
5. Female genitals and
foetus in the uterus
(1510-1512),
Windsor,
Royal Library
(RL 19101r;
K/P 197v).

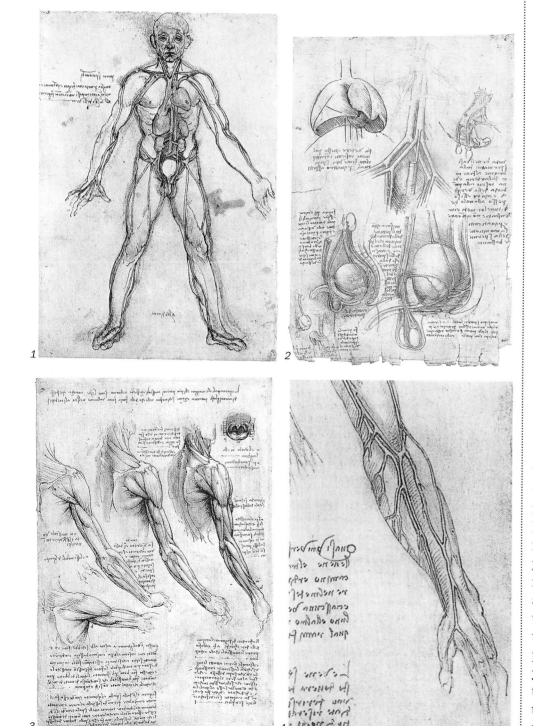

1

2

3

4

"anatomical atlas", similar to Ptole my's *Cosmography*, composed of number of plates illustrating his ex perience on various cadavers, to furnish a tool even more clear and useful than the direct practice of anatomy.

This is obvious from the follow ing proud claim, an extraordinar example of scientific prose of the highest level as well as an avowal of the difficulties, often revolting, en dured by Leonardo in his thirst for knowledge:

«And you who say it is better to see anatomy conducted than to see these drawings, you would be righ if it were possible to see in a single figure all of the things that the drawings show; but with all of your ingenuity in this, you will not see and you will have no knowledge of anything but a few veins [...]. And a single body was not enough for the time required so that it was neces sary to go on to many bodies in or der to have complete knowledge and I did this twice to see the differ ences [...]. And if you are attracted to such a thing you will perhaps be prevented by the stomach, and i this does not prevent you, it will be the fear of spending the hours of the night in the company of such bodies, quartered and skinned and unpleasant to see. And if this does not prevent you, perhaps you will have no gift for drawing, which is needed for such illustration; or, if you have a gift for drawing, it will not be accompanied by perspective; and, if it is, you will be lacking in the order of geometric demonstra tion, or in calculating the forces and power of the muscles, or perhaps you will be lacking in patience, so that you will not be diligent. If all these things have been present in me, the hundred and twenty books

1. *Observer looking into a glass model of the human eye (1508-1509) detail, Manuscript D (3v).*
2. *Lateral views of the skull (c. 1489), Windsor, Royal Library*
(RL 19057r; K/P 43r).
3. *Technique for injecting molten wax into the cerebral ventricles to reveal the inner shape of the brain of an ox (c. 1508-1509), Windsor,*
Royal Library (RL 19127r; K/P 104r).
4. *Section view of a human head (c. 1493-1494), Windsor, Royal Library (RL 12603r; K/P 32r).*
5. *The ventricles, eyeballs with optic nerve and cranial nerves (versus of the so-called Weimar Folio).*

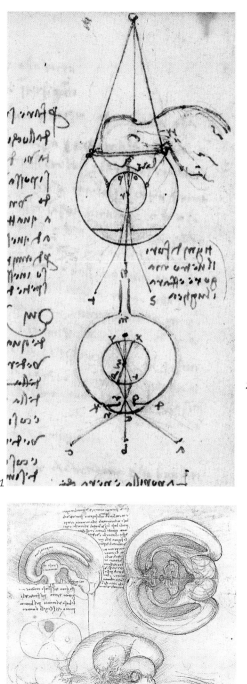

[chapters] composed by me will give judgement, in which I have been impeded neither by avarice nor by negligence, but only by time. Farewell».

THE EYE AND THE BRAIN

Leonardo's first true anatomical studies date from the years 1487-1493, during his stay in Milan. These studies consisted of exploration of the cranium (rendered in the drawings with extraordinary accuracy and perspective) through which Leonardo hoped to find the meeting place of all of the senses, or "common sense", which was also considered the seat of the soul.

The activity of painter and the investigation of nature, based on observation of its phenomena, must have triggered in him interest in the functioning of the eye as the instrument of sight. Already in the early 1490s Leonardo was drawing, following the indications of the ancient authors, eyeballs from which the optic nerves depart for the brain. And in the early 16th century he was still dedicated, but with greater independence, to studying the connections between eye and brain, drawing first the chiasma, or meeting point of the optic nerves.

Leonardo later carried his examination of the ventricles of the brain (not human but bovine) still further by developing an ingenious sculptural technique consisting of injecting melted wax into an organ, allowing it to solidify and then removing it to reveal the shape of that anatomical part.

THE SKELETON AND BONES

Leonardo's interest in osteology (the study of bones) emerged in the years of his maturity, in about 1508-1510, contemporary with other stud-

1. *Bones of the foot and shoulder (1508-1510), Windsor, Royal Library (RL 19011r; K/P 145r).*
2. *The backbone (1508-1509), Windsor,*

Royal Library (RL 19007v; K/P 139v).
3. *Bones of the legs and knee (c. 1508-1510), Windsor, Royal Library (RL 19008r; K/P 140r).*

4. *Movements of the arm determined by the biceps (c. 1508-1510), Windsor, Royal Library (RL 19000v; K/P 135v).*

5. *The skeleton of the trunk and legs (1509-1510), Windsor, Royal Library (RL 19012r; K/P 142r).*

ies conducted directly on the human body, the muscles for example for the purpose of describing their functioning.

In a note written slightly earlier, a memorandum or "commencement" (one of the many) for a treatise on anatomy, Leonardo begins with a reference to the skeleton and the bones as the bearing elements of the human machine: «This instrumental figure of man will be a demonstration in [24] figures, of which the first three will be the ramifications of the bone structure i.e., one will show the latitude of the sites and figures of the bones; the second will appear in profile and will show the depth of all of the parts and their site; the third figure will illustrate the rear part of the bones. Then there will be three other figures of similar aspect, with the bones sectioned, in which their size and inner cavity can be seen».

This note is also useful for understanding the technique of illustration that Leonardo intended to use, consisting of representing the skeleton and each of its individual bones from different angles and at different depths. This can be seen by observing the drawings for this section, rightly considered to rank among Leonardo's finest for their realist anatomical detail as well as for their clearness of line.

MUSCLES AND NERVES

Leonardo's study of the muscular apparatus (myology), conducted mainly between 1505 and 1510, found expression in a series of drawings unanimously acclaimed as among the best and most evocative of the entire anatomical corpus.

The study of muscles proceeded contemporaneous with that of bones and the skeleton, although with sci-

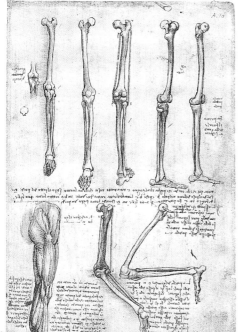

1

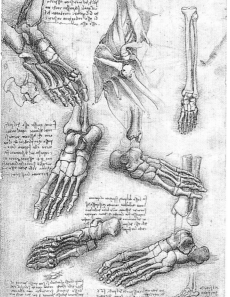

2

3

4

1. Heart of an ox,
Windsor,
Royal Library
(RL 19073-19074v;
K/P 166v).

2. Muscles of the
arm, hand, and face
(1509-1510),
Windsor,
Royal Library
(RL 19012v;
K/P 142v).

3. Muscles of the
neck
(c. 1513),
Windsor,
Royal Library
(RL 19075v;
K/P 179v).

4. The heart
and the lung
(c. 1513),
Windsor,
Royal Library
(RL 19071r;
K/P 162r).

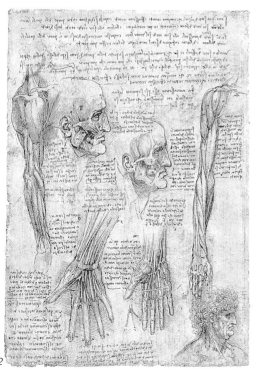

1

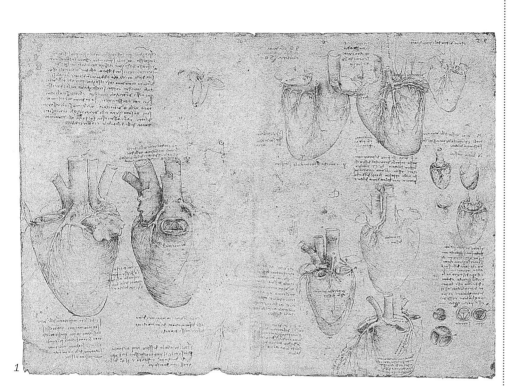

2

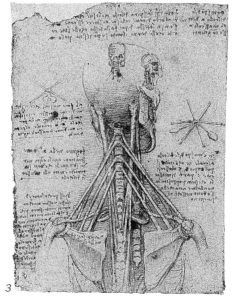

3

entific results not always on the same level, both for the objectively greater difficulty of investigation and for the pioneer nature of studies in myology at the time.

Correlated to the study of the muscles was that of the nerves. After youthful experiments on frogs and monkeys Leonardo made significant progress in the representation of the human central nervous system, drawing the so-called "tree of nerves" which from the brain and the neck extends along the spine from where it branches off to the arms and legs.

THE HEART AND VEINS

Leonardo studied the cardiovascular system at two different times in his life. Dating from the last decade of the 15th century is a drawing depicting "the tree of the veins", strongly influenced by the theories in vogue at the time, the Classical ones of Galenus and the Medieval ones of Mondino.

It was only in later years, around 1513, that Leonardo began to study the heart more thoroughly, experimenting through dissection, although this was done only on animals (mainly oxen) rather than human organs.

But Leonardo was never able to furnish a new, comprehensive, organic idea of the circulatory system, remaining in this substantially bound to the concepts of the Galenic school.

Leonardo exerted great effort to understand the mechanism of the opening and closure of the valves (the aortic valve in particular) and the flow of blood through the heart. To this end he employed again applications and experiments already developed in his activity as hydraulic engineer, when practice in

1. Organs of the chest
   and abdomen of
   a pig (1508-1509),
   Windsor,
   Royal Library
   (RL 19054v;
   K/P 53v).
2. Abdominal viscera
   (1506-1508),
   Windsor,

Royal Library
(RL 19039v and r;
K/P 61v and r).
3. Representation
   of the stomach
   and intestines
   (1506-1508),
   Windsor,
   Royal Library
   (RL 19031v;

K/P 73v).
4. The liver and
   the branches of
   the hepatic veins,
   Windsor,
   Royal Library
   (RL 19051v;
   K/P 60v).
5. Viscera of the chest
   and abdomen with

particular attention
to the heart,
the vascular system
and the lungs
(1506-1508),
Windsor,
Royal Library
(RL 19104v;
K/P 107r).

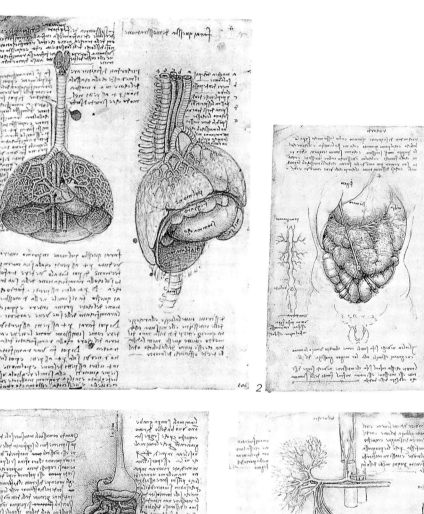

1

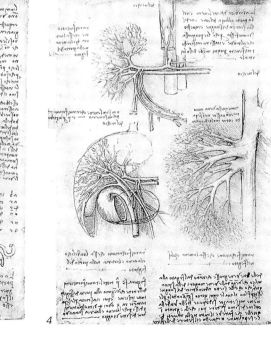

2

3

4

the construction of channels had led him to study attentively phenomena linked to the flow of water. He even constructed a glass model of the aorta, utilising a waxen mould of the artery of an ox through which he passed liquid to conduct experiments on the flow of the blood.

RESPIRATORY, ALIMENTARY AND DIGESTIVE SYSTEMS

Leonardo's observations on the respiratory system are concentrated in the years of his maturity, between 1506 and 1510, and were conducted mainly on animals.

The lungs (of pigs) appear several times in his drawings, represented together with the trachea and the branches of the bronchial tubes and bronchial and pulmonary arteries. Nonetheless, the concept formulated by Leonardo of the respiratory system was not far from that of classical medicine, revived in the Middle Ages, which was limited to declaring the presence of air in the lungs. On the inflow and outflow of this air Leonardo pondered at length, finding no answer.

As regards the alimentary and digestive system, after the rather schematic drawings of his youth Leonardo went on to representing the organs serving these functions with a keen accuracy deriving from his observations on the cadaver of the old man in the winter of 1507-1508.

THE GENITAL ORGANS AND REPRODUCTION

In the case of the genital organs as well, Leonardo went on from a first representation (around 1492-1494) which is quite traditional, although vivacious and expressive, to the extraordinarily accurate one of the years 1510-1512, made famous by a

5

1. *Studies on copulation (c. 1493) detail, Windsor, Royal Library (RL 19097v; K/P 35r).*
2. *Human uterus with foetus (1510-1512), Windsor, Royal Library (RL 19102r; K/P 198r).*
3. *Uterus of a cow seen from the* exterior (above) *and interior (below) (1506-1508), Windsor, Royal Library (RL 19055r; K/P 52r).*
4. *Female genital and urinary system;* ejaculatory canal *(1508), Weimar, Schloss Museum.*
5. *Foetus in the uterus (1510-1512), Windsor, Royal Library (RL 19101r; K/P 197v).*

series of drawings which are justly among the most admired of his entire anatomical corpus.

Important, in the case of woman, is his study of the ovaries and the uterus, represented during pregnancy.

To embryology (the study of the embryo) Leonardo applied himself with particularly brilliant results, although he can frequently be caught in the error of transposing to the human case experiments made on cattle.

We know however that Leonardo had had access, through dissection, to a human foetus of approximately seven months. The drawings show it, in fact, from different points of view, huddled inside the uterus with the umbilical cord that Leonardo describes as being «of the length of the child at each age». In addition to the length and positioning of the umbilical cord, Leonardo was attempting to understand, and with significant results, the miraculous phenomenon that governs the growth and development of the foetus in its mother's womb up to the birth of the new life.

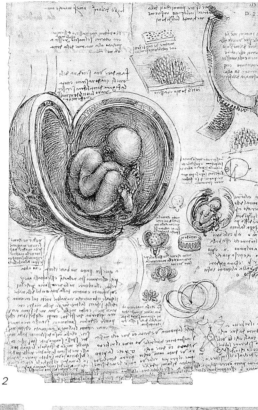

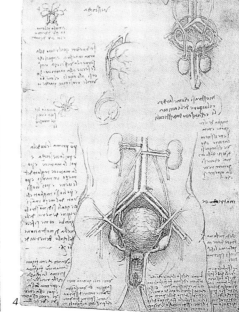

THE BODY IN ART AND IN SCIENCE

The Painter, to be good at portraying the members in all the attitudes and gestures that can be made by nudes, must know the anatomy of the nerves, bones, muscles, and tendons, know for the different movements and forces which nerve or muscle is the cause of such movement, and depict only those, enlarged and evident». So states Leonardo in the *Trattato della pittura*, showing that he considered it necessary for the artist to study anatomy from life, through the practice of dissection. Only in this way could a painter be able to represent the human figure correctly.

While Leonardo's anatomical notebooks are revolutionary for the quality and the intent of the representation as well as for the conception of man as a machine, it is also true that the context in which they were written was mature to welcome such results. The need for a "scientific" portrayal of the human body was perfectly in keeping with the other conquests of Renaissance art. In a space constructed according to scientific rules (arithmetical and perspective), it was only logical and necessary that man should be constructed in equally rigorous manner. And it is precisely this integration between anatomy, proportion and perspective at the service of the representation of the human body which was the true innovation of the Renaissance, when science and art found themselves closely linked and the artist became the crucially important illustrator of what anatomical practice was then discovering. This is why the Renaissance nude, presuming studies in both perspective and anatomy, can be considered the synthesis of this new epoch in art.

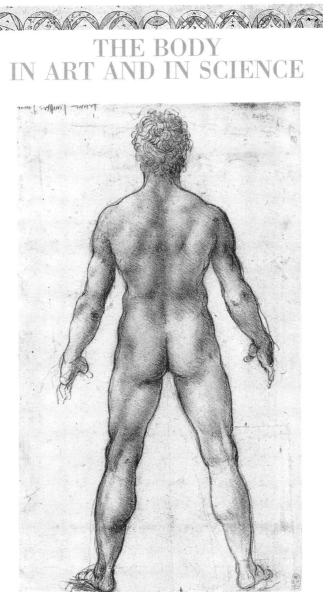

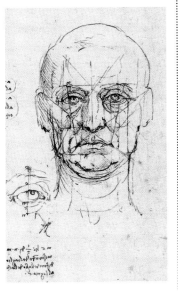

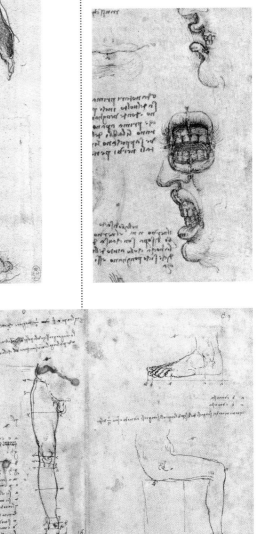

Above, from left:
*study on proportions of the face with details of eyes (c. 1490) detail,
Turin, Biblioteca Reale (no. 15574);
male nude viewed from the back,
Windsor, Royal Library
(K/P 84r; RL 12596r);
studies on muscles of the mouth
(c. 1508) detail,
Windsor,
Royal Library, (RL 19055v).*
At right: *geometric proportions applied to the human figure
(c. 1490), Windsor,
Royal Library
(RL 19136r).*

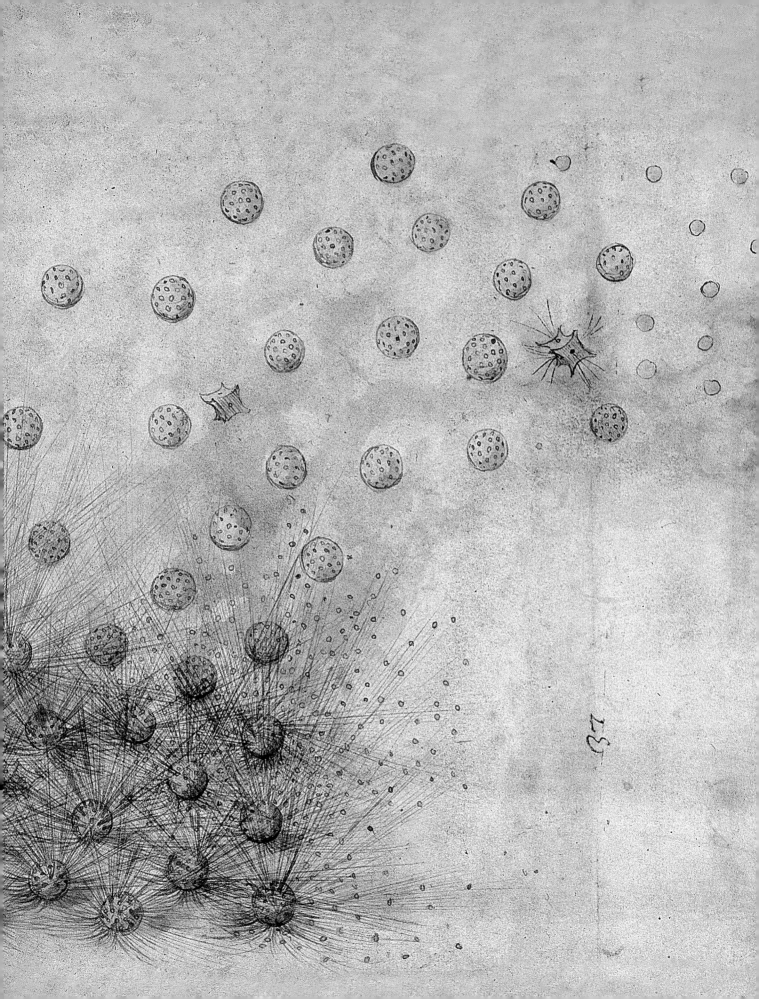

Science and technology

Famed for many decades as the highest manifestation of human genius and invoked as eloquent proof of the freedom from historical limitations of human thought, capable of bounding high above its own time, Leonardo remains today for a vast public a sensational "precursor", a man who surmised centuries in advance the direction that would be taken by science and technology.

This glorified image has been subjected in recent years to progressive revision, still in course, made possible especially by the adoption of stricter criteria for "reading" his work.

Overleaf, on the two preceding pages: mortar with mechanisms for adjusting its range: the cannon-balls, upon hitting the ground, ejected smaller shot,

Codex Atlanticus (fo. 9v-a).
1-4. Series of designs for machines, Manuscript 8937, Madrid, Biblioteca Nacional (ff. 7r, 4r, 81r, 68v).

5. Spring-driven motor (c. 1495), Manuscript I (fo. 14r).
6. Model of spring-driven motor, Florence, Museo di storia della scienza.

7. Studies on solid geometry with a reminder (at centre, above) «Make lenses to see the moon enlarged» (1513-1514), Codex Atlanticus (fo. 518r).

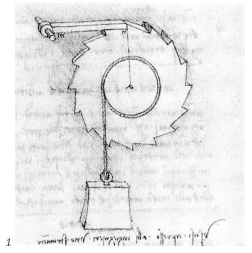

1

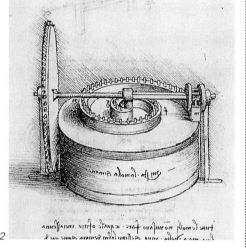

2

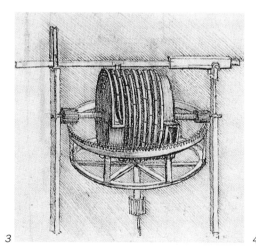

3

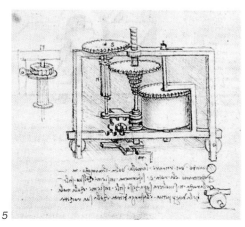

4

5

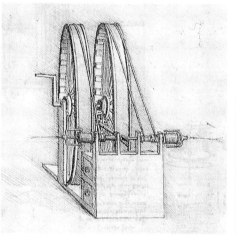

6

In recent years a strong tendency has emerged to tone down the hard-to-die image of Leonardo as misunderstood genius and to emphasise instead the strong evidence of the attention he systematically dedicated to the most advanced experiments and research in the technology of his time. Contemporaneously, it has been noted that Leonardo's career was marked by a number of abrupt, profound changes.

From his apprenticeship with Brunelleschi in the Florence of the 1470s to the attempt to immerse himself in the great texts of classical and contemporary culture during his stay in Milan, the change was significant. Equally significant were the efforts exerted to learn geometry, in the late 15th century and the first decade of the 16th, under the guidance of his friend Luca Pacioli. These powerful efforts exerted in "retraining" also led to a sharp change in the underlying concepts of his technological research which Leonardo increasingly attempted to derive from general scientific bases.

The science of hydraulic engineering dictated the rules for "repairing" rivers. Fluid mechanics, especially the study of the element "air" with its winds and currents, presided over the engineering of flight. A general reflection on "force", "weight" "motion" and "percussion" inspired the analysis of simple mechanisms and thus the engineering of the machines of which they were composed.

Lastly, the "factory" of the human body was subjected to the same mechanical rules through which Leonardo explained the great phenomena that have marked the face of the earth and have contributed over

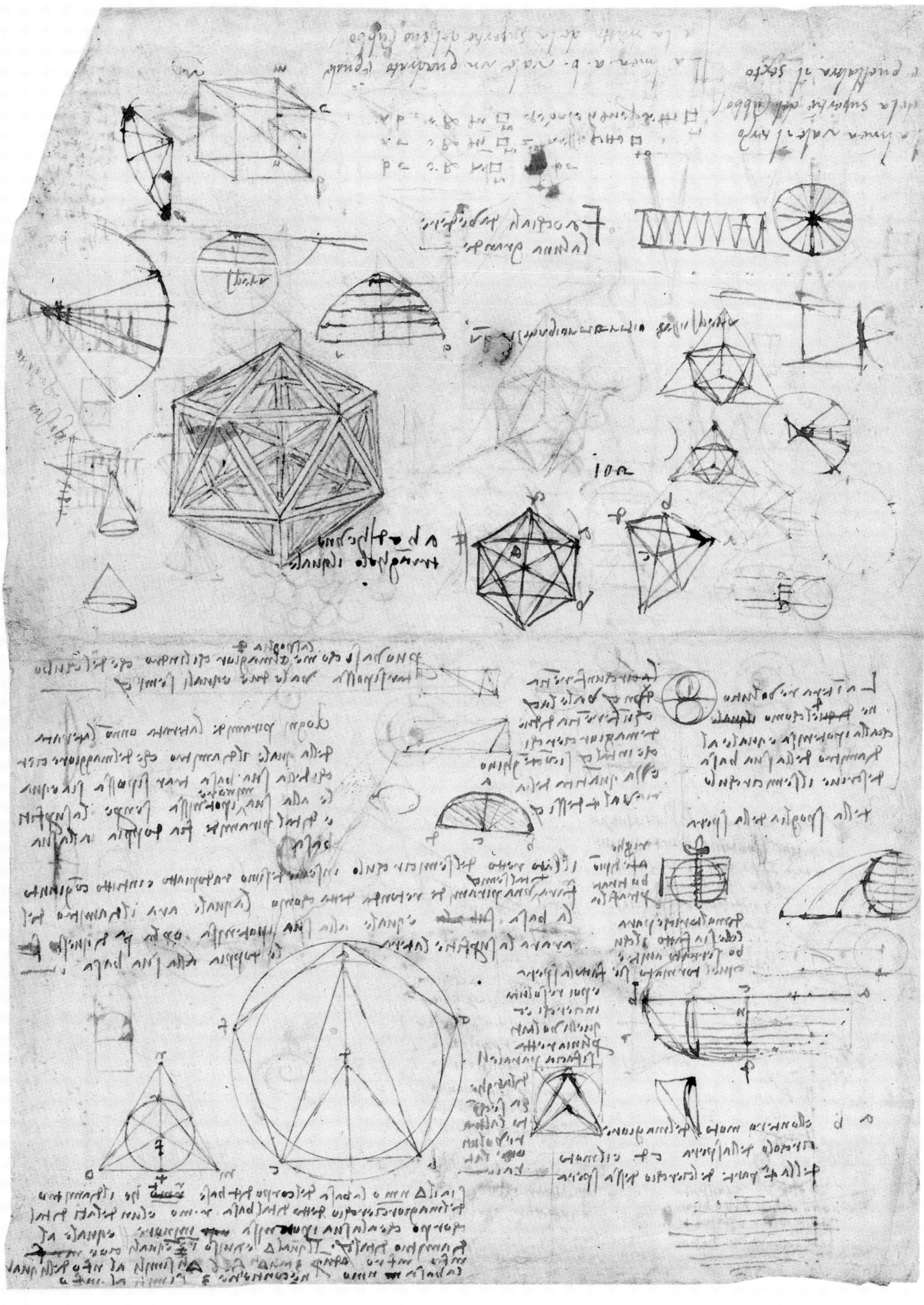

7

1. *Study for a flying machine (the so-called "helicopter") (1487-1490) detail, Manuscript B (fo. 83v).*

2. *Study of life-preserver and fins (1487-1490), Manuscript B (fo. 81v).*

3. *Study of artificial wing (1487-1490), Manuscript B (fo. 74r).*

4. *Method for experimenting the strength of a wing (c. 1487-1490), Manuscript B (fo. 88v).*

5. *Design for ornithopter with pilot in prone position (1487-1490), Manuscript B (fo. 75r).*

the centuries to determining its present-day aspect (mountains and valleys, floods and earthquakes, oceans, springs, and so on).

The effect of this change in attitude on the production of Leonardo the engineer after 1500 is obvious. Isolated technical projects representing an end in themselves, those which were not the direct consequence of vast, ambitious scientific research, become fewer. Vice versa, there was a proportional increase in the frequency of solemn declarations on his intention of dedicating general treatises to great sections of a universal scientific encyclopedia which was at a certain point to absorb most of his energy. The subjects to be treated were water, first of all, the truly universal element, the principal agent of the natural force whose mechanical laws Leonardo was searching for in order to bend it to the service of man; and then motion and weight, anatomy, geometric "transmutations" and all the rest.

Viewed in a chronological perspective, one which shows the evolution of his career, the question - which remains fundamental - of Leonardo's relationship with the other Renaissance engineers takes on a more complex meaning. It now seems that both the traditional sharp contrast between the great inventor and his colleagues and the more recent attempts to confine Leonardo's engineering activity within the limits of practice, procedures and projects already fully developed by contemporary engineers and those of previous generations must be rejected as inadequate.

It has been entirely appropriate to call attention to such great and original engineers as Brunelleschi, Taccola and Francesco di Giorgio Mar-

5

1. *Vertical ornithopter (1487-1490), Manuscript B (fo. 80r).*

2. *Devices for manufacturing concave mirrors (1478-1480), Codex Atlanticus (fo. 17v [4v a]).*

3. *Studies for "battiloro" machine (c. 1493-1495), Codex Atlanticus (fo. 29r).*

4. *Drawings of military machines (1487-1490) Windsor, Royal Library.*

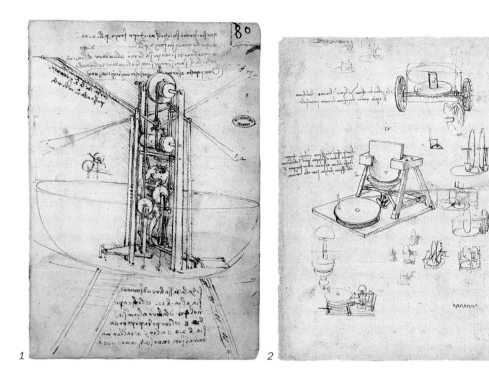

1

2

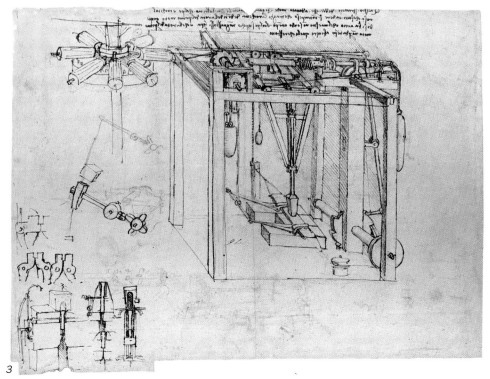

3

tini, esteemed by Leonardo himsel. However, it must not be forgotter that Leonardo, at a certain poin radically changed his own concep of the engineering profession, pro posing to replace a culture foundec on practice and aimed at resolvin, individual cases with a set of uni versal scientific principles on whicl any particular technical solutio must always be strictly based.

Although his dramatic efforts end ed substantially in failure, althoug he never managed to let man reall fly or live and work underwate Leonardo must still be considerec an extraordinary innovator.

THE DRAWING AS DESIGN

Leonardo's originality is to be found expressly in his search for the gen eral mechanical principles whicl govern the operation of any type o machine, rather than in the sensa tional inventions long presented a fabulous precursors.

And Leonardo was original also ir his drawings which, even in their ir completeness, are correctly inter preted as the conceptual equivalen of the "model".

This has been correctly under stood as the meaning of the extraor dinary attention he dedicated to de veloping and defining some excep tional techniques of technologica drawing, thanks to which he man aged to depict not only the ma chines as a whole and their funda mental mechanisms, but also to dia gram their operation.

In this field Leonardo boasts a su premacy which is unrivalled anc which places him at the very begin ning of modern scientific illustra tion. Never before had anyone managed to demonstrate a complex technical design so effectively in a drawing.

4

1. *Wooden model of building reproduced in figure 5, Florence, Museo di storia della scienza.*

2. *Study on thrust of arches for the dome on the Milan Cathedral (c. 1487-1490), Codex Atlanticus (fo. 850r).*

3. *Revolving crane (1478-1480), Codex Atlanticus (fo. 965r).*
4. *Model of revolving crane, Florence, Museo di storia della scienza.*

5. *Study for church with central plan (1487-1490), Manuscript B (fo. 95r).*

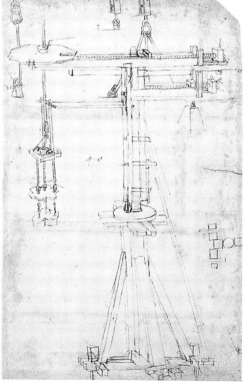

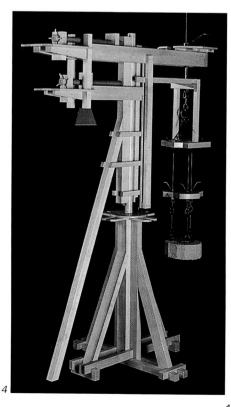

LEONARDO AS ARCHITECT

Leonardo was not and did not claim to be an architect, although he furnished, and above all made drawings of, architectural models. The nature of his work is clear only in a few circumstances, such as in the case of the design for the dome on the Milan Cathedral, in 1488-1490 or that of the villa commissioned him by the Governor of the Duchy of Milan Charles d'Amboise in about 1506-1508; or again in that of 1516-1517 for the castle of Romorantin at the request of the King of France, François I.

But his most prodigious contribution to the development of a new architecture all over Italy cannot be clearly defined. The same difficulty, moreover, was announced by Vasari already in 1550. After having proclaimed the Leonardo's supremacy in the field of painting he continues: «Not one profession alone did he practice but all those involving drawing. And he had an intellect so divine and marvelous that, being an excellent geometer, not only did he work in sculpture and in architecture, but declared painting to be his own profession». He added a significant addition in the edition published in 1568: «But in architecture he still made many drawings, of both plans and other buildings, and was again the first who, as a young man, spoke of the Arno river and of channeling it from Pisa to Florence».

This having been said, the most interesting thing is perhaps to understand the place held by Leonardo in the "architectural culture" of the age, his relations with contemporaries and predecessors.

In alternative to ancient texts translated and commented for him (Bramante and Pacioli were always

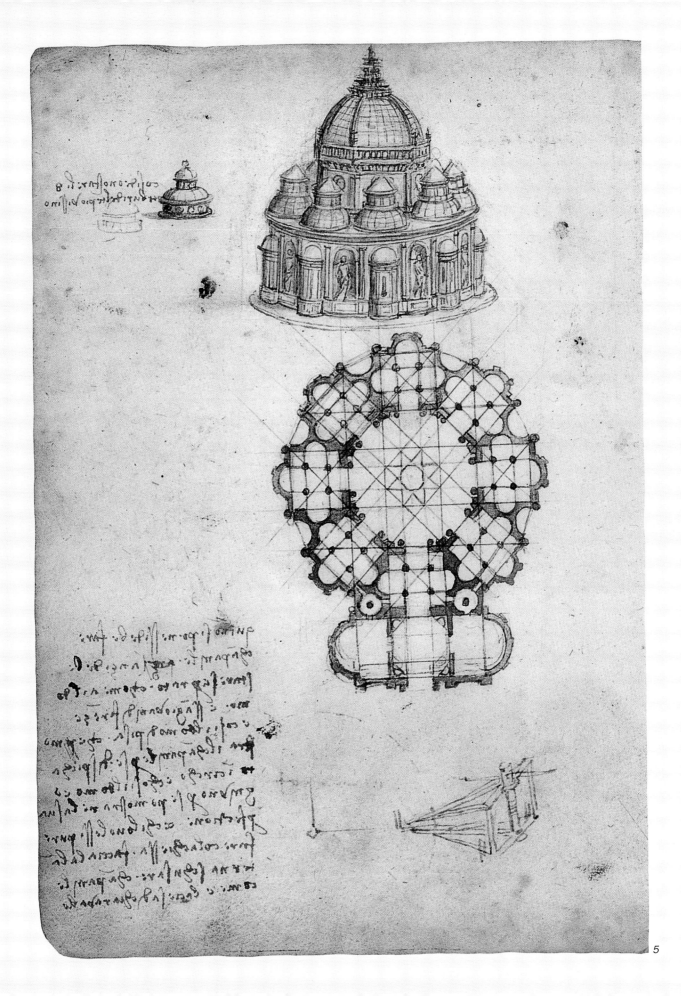

5

1. Imaginary reconstruction of an Etruscan tomb, with view of exterior, plan and subterranean chamber, Louvre (no. 2386).

2. Studies of churches with circular plan, of reverberatory furnaces and of a "tool with spheres", i.e., one for manufacturing burning mirrors (1487-1490), Manuscript B (fo. 21v).

3. Bird's eye view of a fortress (c. 1504), Manuscript 8936 (fo. 79r), Madrid, Biblioteca Nacional.

1

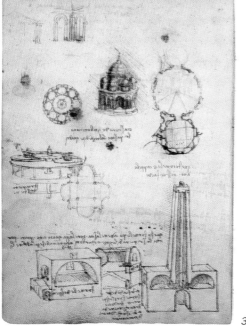

2

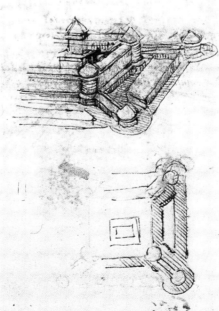

3

nearby, in Milan), Leonardo turned to the contemporary works of Francesco di Giorgio Martini, a copy of whose *Trattato di architettura civile e militare* he annotated Codex Madrid II, for example, contains the project for a fortified body with ravelins (fo. 79r) unquestionably derived expressly from Francesco di Giorgio Martini. There are also quotations in the *Trattato* referring to working diagrams.

Nor should the influence of Giuliano da Sangallo, who was also in Milan in 1492 for the matter of the cathedral dome, be underestimated. But it is to Brunelleschi first of all that we must look to understand the formulation of Leonardo's ideas on architecture. The legacy of Brunelleschi had been thoroughly asimilated at the time of Leonardo's "polytechnical" apprenticeship in Verrocchio's workshop. Not only the sublime octagon of the dome on Santa Maria del Fiore and the pure rhythms of the Florentine basilicas, but also the apparatus of machines, winches, lifts, levers and building formulas whose example was under the eyes of all. The entire reflection on the central plan, which was to take shape in about 1490 with the admirable small design of an octagon with radially chapel, is manifestly derived from Brunelleschi's example.

Concerning Leon Battista Alberti instead, a strange silence reigns over the work of Leonardo. It is perhaps inevitable to accept the conviction that he wished to avoid the example of a declared disciple of Vitruvius and of classicism such as Alberti. And it was in fact in Milan, with Bramante and Pacioli, in a new environment, "freer" than that of Florence, that Leonardo was to find his path.

Historical research has now verified that among the ancient texts re-introduced to the western culture of the Humanists in the 15th century, those of Archimedes were decisively important in favouring a true "rebirth" of science, based on strictly geometrical and mathematical principles, destined to produce revolutionary results at the close of the 16th century with Galileo. Already in the late 15th century, however, Archimedes was a mandatory reference point in scientific debate. His works were studied both in the Greek text (which Poliziano had copied at Venice for the Libreria Medicea in a volume that belonged Lorenzo Valla) and in the Latin versions: the Medieval one of Moerbeke and the Renaissance one of Iacopo da Cremona.

Like the other great engineers of the Renaissance (Francesco di Giorgio Martini, Alberti and, later, Tartaglia), Leonardo felt the need to return to Archimedes, leaving evidence of intense study of his writings. It is certain that he could consult the *Dimensio Circuli* published by Gaurico in 1504. He was acquainted with the *Equilibrio dei Piani e dei Galleggianti* (transcribed in part in the Codex Atlanticus).

In Leonardo's texts, the Syracusan scientist shows the dual nature conferred on him by tradition: the very concrete aspect of engineer-inventor (burning mirrors to set fire to the Roman ships; «screws» for lifting; the «architronite», a steam cannon the invention of which Leonardo attributes to him; a system for detecting the ruse of the swindler who had sold for gold to Gerone, the tyrant of Syracuse, a crown made instead of gold

AND I CAN SQUARE THE CIRCLE

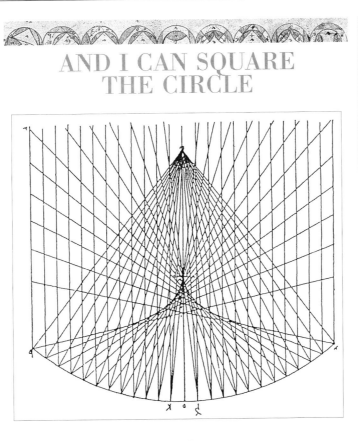

Above: *Studies on reflection causistics inspired by Archimedes' burning mirrors (c. 1508), Codex Arundel (fo. 87v).*

Below: *Studies of parabolic mirrors for exploiting solar energy (c. 1513-1515), Codex Atlanticus (fo. 750r).*

and silver alloy); and the contrasting aspect of "Platonizer", absent-minded scientist, incapable of abandoning his contemplation of geometric bodies even while the Romans were invading Syracuse, and thus paying with his life

for his love of truth.

It is probably in relation to the concept of Archimedes as engineer and inventor that Leonardo's name was recorded in the Gaurico edition of Archimedes' writings (where Leonardo is called «famous for

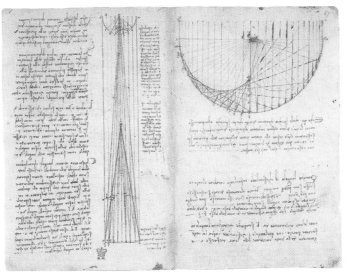

his Archimedean genius»).

However, many passages by Leonardo testify to his admiration for the Syracusan scientist's knowledge of geometry. This admiration, although enormous, never took the form of passive imitation.

Leonardo carefully considered Archimedes' solutions to the problems of squaring the circle and to curvilinear figures, pointing out the aspects he found inadequate: Archimedes' squaring of the circle was well stated and badly done». Archimedes had squared not a circle but «a figura laterata», while Leonardo believed he himself had gone further: «And I can square the circle, except for a portion as minimal as the mind can imagine, i.e., the visible point».

Elsewhere Leonardo announces that he has found, on November 30, 1504, the solution to the age-old problem of squaring the circle: «On the night of St. Andrew I found the end of the squaring of the circle at the end of the lamp-light and of the night and of the paper I was writing on; it was concluded at the end of the hour». Unfortunately, no trace of this presumed solution remains.

Leonardo's intense reflections on squaring the circle are not one of the most interesting and original aspects of his scientific activity. But for Leonardo, as for many of his contemporaries, the return to Archimedes represented not merely the chance to find an answer to some of the great problems of geometry, but above all the discovery of a method of geometrical/mechanical investigation of reality that was to bring about a radical transformation in the very way in which scientific knowledge was understood.

CHRONOLOGY

1452

Leonardo is born at Vinci on April 15, the natural son of the notary Ser Piero di Antonio da Vinci.

At Arezzo, in the Church of San Francesco, Piero della Francesca begins the cycle of frescoes known as the *Legend of the True Cross*.

1454

The Peace of Lodi inaugurates a period of political stability in Italy.

1469

Leonardo presumably enters Verrocchio's workshop in this year.

1472

He is enrolled in the painters' association, the Compagnia di San Luca. His first works start from this date: costumes and sets for festivals and jousts, a cartoon for a tapestry (lost) and the paintings of uncertain dating.

1473

He dates (August 5) the drawing of the *Landscape of the Val d'Arno* (Florence, Uffizi Gallery).

1476

Accused of sodomy along with other persons, he is acquitted.

In Milan Galeazzo Maria Sforza is assassinated in a plot. His son Gian Galeazzo succeeds him; the city is governed by Simonetta.

1478

Leonardo is commissioned to paint the altarpiece for the Chapel of San Bernardo in Palazzo della Signoria. In this same year he states that he has completed two paintings of the Virgin, one of which is now identified as the *Benois Madonna*.

The Pazzi Conspiracy, fomented by Pope Sixtus IV, fails. Giuliano de' Medici dies, but the authority of his brother Lorenzo the Magnificent is reinforced.

1480

According to the "Anonimo Gaddiano", Leonardo works for Lorenzo de' Medici.

Ludovico Sforza kills Simonetta, imprisons his nephew and illicitly becomes the lord of Milan.

1481

Contract for the *Adoration of the Magi*.

1482

Leonardo moves to Milan leaving the *Adoration of the Magi* unfinished.

1483

In Milan Leonardo stipulates the contract for the *Virgin of the Rocks* in collaboration with Evangelista and Ambrogio De Predis.

Raphael is born in Urbino.

1487

Payment for projects for the lantern on the Milan Cathedral.

1488

Verrocchio dies in Venice, where he was completing the equestrian monument to Colleoni. Bramante is in Pavia as consultant for designing the Cathedral.

1489

Leonardo designs sets for the festivities celebrating the wedding of Gian Galeazzo Sforza and Isabella d'Aragon. In this same year he begins preparations for the colossal equestrian statue in honor of Francesco Sforza.

1491

Giangiacomo Caprotti da Oreno, known as "Salai", enters Leonardo's service. The nickname "Salai", which means "devil", derives from the boy's unruly character.

1492

For the wedding of Ludovico il Moro and Beatrice d'Este, Leonardo designs the costumes for the parade of Scythians and Tartars.

In Florence Lorenzo de' Medici dies. The system of alliances sanctioned by the Peace of Lodi begins to break up.

1494

Land reclamation work on one of the Duke's estates near Vigevano.

The King of France Charles VIII, allying himself with Ludovico il Moro, invades Italy to claim his right to the Kingdom of Naples.

1495

Leonardo begins the *Last Supper* and the decoration of rooms in the Castello Sforzesco. The artist's name is mentioned as Ducal Engineer.

1497

The Duke of Milan urges the artist to finish the *Last Supper*, which is probably completed by the end of the year.

1498

Leonardo completes the decoration of the Sala delle Asse in the Castello Sforzesco.

Pollaiolo dies in Rome, where he has designed the tombs of Sixtus IV and Innocent VIII. Michelangelo is commissioned to sculpt the *Pietà* in St. Peter's. In Florence Savonarola is burned at the stake.

1499

Leonardo leaves Milan in the company of Luca Pacioli. Stops first at Vaprio to visit the Melzi family, then leaves for Venice passing through Mantua, where he draws two portraits of Isabella d'Este.

Luca Signorelli begins the frescoes in the Chapel of San Brizio in the Orvieto Cathedral. Milan is occupied by the King of France, Louis XII.

1500

_eonardo arrives in Venice in March. Returns
o Florence where he resides in the Monastery of the Servite Brothers in the Santissi-
na Annunziata.

n Florence, Piero di Cosimo paints the *Sto-
ies of Primitive Humanity*.

1502

_eonardo enters the service of Cesare Bor-
gia as architect and general engineer, follo-
ving him on his military campaigns through
Romagna.

n Rome, Bramante begins the Tempietto di
San Pietro in Montorio and the Belvedere
Courtyard.

1503

_eonardo returns to Florence where, accord-
ng to Vasari, he paints the *Mona Lisa*. De-
vises projects for deviating the course of the
Arno River during the siege of Pisa. Commissioned by the Signoria to paint the *Battle of Anghiari*.

1504

Continues to work on the *Battle of Anghiari*.
Is called upon to participate in the commission that will decide where to place Michelangelo's *David*. First studies for the *Leda and the Swan*.

Michelangelo completes the *David* commis-
sioned from him three years before by the
Republic of Florence. Raphael paints the
Marriage of the Virgin; then moves to Flo-
rence, where he is profoundly influenced by
Leonardo's work.

1506

Leonardo leaves Florence for Milan, planning
to return within three months. The stay in Milan extends beyond this time.

1508

Leonardo is in Florence, then returns to Milan.

In Rome, Michelangelo commits himself to
frescoing the ceiling of the Sistine Chapel.
In Venice, Giorgione and Titian fresco the
Fondaco dei Tedeschi.

1509

Geological studies on the valleys of Lombardy.

Raphael is in Rome, where he begins deco-
rating the *Stanze*.

1510

Studies on anatomy with Marcantonio della
Torre at the University of Pavia.

1512

Michelangelo completes the frescoes on the
ceiling of the Sistine Chapel. The Sforza return to Milan.

1513

Leonardo leaves Milan for Rome, where he
lives in the Vatican Belvedere under the protection of Giuliano de' Medici. Remains in
this city for three years, engaged in mathematical and scientific studies.

Pope Julius II dies. He is succeeded by Giovanni de' Medici under the name of Leo X.
In Florence, Andrea del Sarto begins the cycle of frescoes *Stories of the Virgin*. In Milan, Cesare da Sesto with his *Baptism of
Christ* achieves a synthesis of the style of
Leonardo and that of Raphael.

1514

Projects for draining the Pontine swamps
and for the port of Civitavecchia.

In Rome Bramante dies. Raphael succeeds
him as architect of the Fabric of St. Peter's.

1515

Francis I becomes King of France. With the
victory of Marignano he reconquers Milan.
Raphael works on the cartoons for the tape-
stries in the Sistine Chapel.

1516

Charles of Hapsburg becomes King of Spain.

1517

Leonardo moves to Amboise, to the court of
Francis I, King of France. In mid-January he
visits Romorantin with the King to plan a new
royal residence and a system of canals in
the region of Sologne.

In Rome, Raphael and his assistants paint
the "Logge" in the Vatican and the Loggia of
Psyche in the Villa Farnesina.

1518

Leonardo participates in the festivities for the
baptism of the Dauphin and for the wedding
of Lorenzo de' Medici to the King's niece.

1519

On April 23 Leonardo writes his will. The exe-
cutor is his friend the painter Francesco
Melzi. He dies on May 2. In the burial cer-
tificate, dated August 12, he is described as
a «noble Milanese, first painter and engineer
and architect to the King, State Mechanical
Engineer».

Charles V of Hapsburg is elected Emperor of
the Holy Roman Empire. Open conflict breaks
out between France and the Empire. In Parma, Correggio paints the Badessa's Chamber in the Convent of San Paolo.

INDEX

Numbers in bold refer to images.